The Authority of Divine Love

Faith and the Future
General Editor: David Nicholls

Choices
Ethics and the Christian
David Brown

Church and Nation
Peter Cornwell

Pastoral Care and the Parish
Peter Davie

The Faith Abroad
John D. Davies

Church, Ministry and Unity
A Divine Commission
James E. Griffiss

The Authority of Divine Love
Richard Harries

The Bible
Fountain and Well of Truth
John Muddiman

Faith, Prayer and Devotion
Ralph Townsend

Sacraments and Liturgy
The Outward Signs
Louis Weil

The Authority of Divine Love

Richard Harries

Basil Blackwell

First published 1983
Basil Blackwell Publisher Limited
108 Cowley Road, Oxford OX4 1JF, England

British Library Cataloguing in Publication Data

Harries, Richard
The authority of divine love.–(Faith and the future)
1. Authority (Religion)
I. Title II. Series
262'.8 BT88

ISBN 0–631–13205–8
ISBN 0–631–13228–7 Pbk

Typeset by Cambrian Typesetters,
Aldershot, Hants
Printed in Great Britain by
T.J. Press Ltd, Padstow

For colleagues and friends at
All Saints', Fulham, 1972–81

David Tann
Peter Kaye
Peter Wheatley
Christopher Moody
Stephen Wilson

By the same author

Prayers of Hope
Turning to Prayer
Prayers of Grief and Glory
Being a Christian
Should a Christian support Guerillas?
What Hope in an Armed World? (ed.)
Praying Round the Clock

Contents

Foreword

This book is one of a series whose writers consider some important aspects of Christianity in the contemporary scene and in so doing draw inspiration from the Catholic revival in the Anglican Communion which began in Oxford one hundred and fifty years ago. This revival – with its thinkers, pastors, prophets, social reformers and not a few who have been held to be saints – has experienced changes in the understanding of the Christian faith since the time of the Tractarians and has nonc the less borne witness to themes which are deep and unchanging. Among these are the call to holiness, the communion of saints, the priesthood of the Church and its ministers and a sacramental religion, both otherworldly and with revolutionary claims upon man's social life.

I am myself convinced that the renewal of the Church for today and tomorrow needs a deep recovery of these themes of Catholic tradition and a vision of their contemporary application. The books of this series are designed towards this end, and I am sure that readers will be grateful for the help they give. Many are thirsty but 'the well is deep'.

+ Michael Ramsey

Acknowledgements

I am grateful to the Reverend Dr David Nicholls, The Reverend Dr John Halliburton and Father Michael Richards SJ for reading the typescript and for making some useful comments.

Richard Harries
King's College, London

1 Authority — a Dangerous but Essential Idea

> If people were now asked what was the most powerful means of advancing the cause of religion in the world, we should be told that it was eloquence of speech or preaching . . . Whereas, if we were to judge from Holy Scripture, of what were the best means of promoting Christianity in the world, we should say obedience; and if we were to be asked the second, we should say obedience; and if we were to be asked the third, we should say obedience.

This passage by Isaac Williams, a poet and friend of John Henry Newman, appeared in the 87th of a series of 90 tracts, or statements of belief in pamphlet form, which defined the position of the Oxford Movement in its early stages. The passage well represents the attitude of the Oxford Movement (or 'Tractarians', as they were called), an attitude that regarded authority and its concomitant, obedience, as indispensable for both society and the Church. There were many controversies surrounding authority, but they did not doubt that authority was necessary or that obedience was a virtue. We do. Four reasons are suggested to account for our suspicion of any stress on the importance of authority or the desirability of obedience.

First, what happened in Germany in the 1930s still serves as a terrible warning. Within Lutheran thought there is a consistent emphasis on the authority of the state and the necessity of obedience to it. St Paul's words in Romans 13 hold a central place. Many people now believe that this emphasis created a soil in which it was possible for the noxious weed of Nazism to flourish much more rapidly than would otherwise have been the case. The 'good German' was one who gave an unquestioning obedience to the state and its institutions. This helped to blind people to the evil that was growing up around them, and made them reluctant to act against it. What happened in Germany remains, and rightly remains, part of the cultural air we breathe, leading to a suspicion of any stress on authority, whether in religion or politics.

Secondly, while the Marxist analysis of society taken as a whole is false, it nevertheless contains insights which have been widely recognized as true. One such insight is that the values a person or group champions are likely to be related to their socio-economic position. So, for example, while most people admit that society should be characterized by both justice and order, in practice certain kinds of people will be found calling for greater social justice, and others will be urging that more money be spent on forces of law and order. A man perched precariously at the top of a pile of badly stacked logs will call for stability. But a man squashed under the pile won't worry about the consequences of an upheaval. He wants the weight off his back, and will cry for freedom. This does not mean that values are simply a product of social forces; they are not. But which particular values are emphasized, and by whom, cannot be isolated from social and economic considerations. It is obvious therefore that the necessity of obedience to authority will be stressed most by those who have the biggest stake in a society and regarded with most suspicion by those who have least to lose if the society disintegrates. So if the importance of authority is emphasized by the powerful and wealthy, and the Church acts as their ally, people are understandably sceptical. Although both this and the previous reason are concerned with political life, they tend to make people suspicious of authority in all its forms.

Thirdly, there is a suspicion derived from a general observation of human personalities and from the work of psychoanalysts. Certain people are more authoritarian than others, more rigid both in relation to themselves and to other people. In Freudian theory this is connected with the presence of a fierce super-ego and a fear of strong emotions that are present but only partially recognized. Again, deriving in part from the work of analysts and therapists, an alternative model or ideal of personality is widely accepted in the West. This is one in which the emotions are honestly faced, in which people are characterized by openness to and acceptance of the often turbulent forces within; and so accept the similar forces within other people.

Fourthly, in conscious opposition to authoritarian models of political and personal life an alternative ideal has been developed. In secular life there has been an emphasis on personal freedom, expressed in much modern literature, such as the works of Jean Paul Sartre. For him personal choice is an inescapable burden and a responsibility which must be accepted even when the individual is confronted by a person or institution claiming authority. In church life this emphasis on freedom takes the form of stressing that every Christian has his or her own charism, or gift of the spirit; in a sharing by lay people in the government of the Church at every level; in an emphasis on collegiality between pope and bishops, and so on. The Church is now seen by many not as an institution marked by hierarchy and obedience but as a brotherhood of equals, all endowed by the spirit and all participating in the life of the body. This positive ideal, which many parishes and individuals are seeking to realize, erodes models in which authority plays a key role.

These suspicions of authority must be taken with the utmost seriousness, and there can be no rehabilitation of the notion of authority without doing justice to them. But it also must be asserted unequivocally that the Christian faith cannot do without some concept of authority. There are simple reasons for this. God exists and has revealed his mind and purpose to us. An interesting contrast in this respect can be made with Hinduism. It has been said that

Hinduism is not a religion in the sense that we understand the word, as it consists of literally thousands of highly diverse forms. There is nothing that can be pointed to as that which constitutes and defines the essentially Hindu element in all these different forms of worship and belief. They have evolved without any direction from central authority, each with their own set of sacred scriptures. In contrast Judaism, Christianity and Islam are all based on a belief that there is one God and that he has revealed himself to us. In these three religions there is a body of sacred scripture which seeks to enshrine and safeguard the revelation and which is regarded as authoritative.

Yet this is not enough upon which to rest a doctrine of authority. For it would be quite possible, and rightly possible, for a person to be told that there is a God and that this God has disclosed himself to us and to reply 'so what?'. The remarkable French philosopher, Simone Weil, wrote at one point that Christ could die and rise again in front of her several times and it would make no difference to her acceptance of Christian teaching. This highlights what is missing from the reason already adduced: the moral element. Before acknowledging someone's authority we must first recognize the moral worth of that authority. It would be possible for there to be a God who first created the world and then revealed his purpose to mankind, but who was hostile or indifferent to human welfare. For God to have our allegiance it is necessary not only that he exists and discloses himself to us but also that we judge him to be worthy of our highest moral and spiritual response. The word 'worthy' sounds prosaic, but worship really means 'worth-ship'. Genuine worship is rooted in a recognition of the supreme worth of God as the source and standard of all that we value.

So the idea of authority is taken seriously by Christians not just because God exists and because he has revealed himself to us, but also because we see in that revelation the mind and heart of love. The Christian faith is rooted in that recognition. The love of God revealed in Christ has two aspects which, in contrast to our own human love, reinforce the importance of authority in the Christian life. God's love is for every single person who lives, has lived, or will live. His purpose embraces the whole of mankind. In contrast to this we are aware how limited and partial our own outlook is. We find it difficult to widen the circle of our concern much beyond our own family. God's love for us is also perfect, without any blemish of selfishness or self-preoccupation; he is clear-sighted, wholehearted and unceasing in his work for our well-being. In contrast to this even our love of ourselves is blighted. We hardly know what is for our own good, half-heartedly desire it and only weakly work for it. God, who is perfect love, knows our good, desires it ardently and is using every device of infinite wisdom, power and patience to bring it about. In short he loves us infinitely more than we love ourselves. These considerations can only reinforce the indispensable role of authority in the Christian life. Conscious of our limited outlook and feeble capacity to love, we open ourselves to God.

I have suggested several reasons why people feel suspicious of the notion of authority. But the abuse of an idea does not mean that the whole idea should be jettisoned. After the world's experience of Hitler and the Nazis steps were taken to forearm people in case such a situation should arise again. Within Lutheranism Helmut Thielicke in his massive *Theological Ethics*[1] has reminded people that Romans 13 is not the only passage in the Bible dealing with government. Revelation 13 reveals that it is possible for a government to become demonic, and declares that if a state usurps to itself the functions of God, it no longer has any authority over Christians. In other Christian traditions there has always been more stress on the right to resist or rebel against tyrannical governments.

In relation to the connection between values and class, it remains true that certain moral and political values are essential for all human communities, however much they may be misused by particular groups of people to serve their own purposes. This misuse is often unconscious; indeed, most people are unaware of the social forces which condition and sweep them along. The fact that the notion of authority has been used to buttress the position of the powerful alerts us to this danger, but it does not mean that the concept has to be abandoned altogether. Even in its most extreme form, the 'divine right' of kings, the kings were still responsible to an ultimate authority, God. In contrast to this, the self-selecting elite who act in the name of the proletariat are accountable only to future historians. At a personal level, however important it is for people to be in touch with their own emotions, we still need a 'super-ego'. We imbibe, and need to imbibe, at a pre-rational level, some basic moral axioms. This is just as necessary for the development of the personality as is a healthy emotional life. Experience of church life suggests that however much emphasis there is, rightly, on participation by all members in the life of the body of Christ, it is necessary to have some focus of authority as well as some decision-making machinery, whereby conflicting expectations and interests can be reconciled and harmonized.

The importance the Christian faith attaches to the notion of authority arises from its conviction that God has revealed himself to us. We do not believe what we believe simply because we have chosen to interpret the universe in a particular way; our belief is a response to what God has made known of himself. But this does not mean that the Christian faith is isolated from other forms of knowledge and ways of knowing. On the contrary; all knowing involves accepting some things on authority. In whatever tradition we grow up as children, whether it is atheism or Roman Catholicism, we begin by accepting what is taught us. Newman put the point forcibly in relation to the Christian faith, but what he wrote applies equally to growing up with other world-views. 'Everyone must begin religion by faith, not by reasoning; he must take for granted what is taught and what he cannot prove; and it is better for himself that he should do so, even if the teaching he receives contains a mixture of error. If he would possess a reverent mind, he must begin by obeying; if he would cherish a generous and devoted spirit, he must begin by venturing somewhat on uncertain information.'[2] 'Under whatever system a man finds himself, he is bound to accept it as if infallible, and to act upon it in a confiding spirit, till he finds a better, or in course of time has cause to suspect it.'[3]

If we begin by questioning everything, we shall never really know anything. A certain openness and receptivity is a condition of learning. What Newman termed 'a reverent mind' and 'a generous and devoted spirit' are not simply desirable moral qualities, nor on the other hand can they be dismissed as tools only used to turn people into dupes and slaves. They are the qualities which make all learning possible. As the philosopher Wittgenstein wrote, 'The child learns by believing the adult. Doubt comes *after* belief.' Again, 'If you tried to doubt everything, you would not get as far as doubting anything. The game of doubting itself presupposes a certainty.'[4]

What is true of a child beginning to learn, and of faith, is no less true within any scientific community. The contrast sometimes made between the always-critical doubting mind of the scientist and the accepting, unquestioning mind of the religious believer is a travesty of the true situation. All scientific learning takes place on the basis of an acceptance of certain fundamentals. Some of these may come to be questioned, but they cannot all be questioned at the same time. A scientist pioneering some research in a specialist field inevitably accepts on authority much of the knowledge upon which he works. Furthermore – and this is a point which also applies more widely – all questioning, argument, thesis and counter-thesis presuppose a common language; and this shared world of discourse is based upon certain assumptions, values and facts which are taken as given.

Our age still suffers from a false individualism. We tend to a romantic image of each individual sitting on his rock in the middle of the ocean agonizing in lonely isolation about fundamental questions of belief and value. This picture is unreal. The true situation is that we are born and brought up in a culture which shapes our thinking from the start. We come, rightly, to question parts of that outlook, or even the outlook as a whole. But even then, in the most extreme rejection of received beliefs and values, the language we use presupposes something in common with what we are questioning, something we are at that point accepting on authority. The great strength of *Believing in the Church*, the report of the Church of England Doctine Commission published in 1981, is expressed in its subtitle, *The corporate nature of faith*. The report reminds us that the adventure of faith, like the scientific enterprise, is inescapably corporate. The Bishop of Winchester writes of tradition as 'more than the deposit of past convictions and formulations. We see it as a still continuing process of *corporate believing*, a patrimony to be reinvested in each generation.'[5] What is perhaps surprising about this valuable book is that it contains not one reference to John Henry Newman, even though his spirit and outlook permeates the whole. He too was concerned about the excessive individualism of the age in which he lived. He was worried particularly by the claims of so many Christians, each of whom asserted that he or she had discovered the true essence or meaning or interpretation of the faith, each discovery differing from the others. Newman directed people to the Church in its corporate aspect, in particular to the undivided Church of the first centuries, and said in effect: there is the faith of the Church; there is the Christian faith. There is that by which we must judge our private opinions. To be a Christian means standing in that tradition and belonging to the living extension of that community.

The Christian understanding of authority arises from its unique claim that God has revealed himself in Jesus, but it does not stand alone. The scientific research worker, no less than the Christian, belongs to a community in which the acceptance of much on authority is the indispensable precondition of the whole enterprise.

Today Christians concerned about authority face a new danger: a new authoritarianism. This is partly simply a fashionable reaction. The 1960s saw a great explosion against any kind of authority, the 1970s saw a creeping conservatism, and the 1980s show signs of a deepening reaction of which the so-called 'moral majority' in America is only one symptom. Changes of fashion are inevitable, and if one is aware of what is happening, not too dangerous. But our time is characterized by great uncertainties. Urbanization, the break-up of the traditional family unit and the lack of community are just some of the social factors which make people look for, and try to cling to, something they can regard as absolutely certain. One of the signs of a declining civilization is the mushrooming of all kinds of religious cults. Amid the political and economic insecurities of the Roman world in the second and third centuries, gnostic cults and religions of many other kinds abounded. Our own period, far from being 'secular', is similar. Some of these cults and religions appeal because they offer mystery, secret knowledge, something esoteric. The more dangerous kind are authoritarian and verge on brainwashing. The next twenty years is likely to see a great rise in the influence of religions of all kinds, and many of these will be authoritarian in character. In a world where so many people feel insecure and rootless, where society is not held together by an overarching sense of purpose, anyone who gets up and speaks confidently enough will get a hearing and adherents. It is very easy to talk and write confidently, and there will be many people willing to use this ploy to bring people into bondage to authoritarian religious systems.

In this situation, faced with this kind of danger, the Christian wants to assert that the only true basis for authority is a divine love that calls forth our wholehearted moral assent. We are moral beings, and in the end the only reason for giving our allegiance to something is not that it is more powerful, more confident or more guilt-inducing, but simply that it is the fount and focus of all that we value. God's power by itself does not avail, nor does the fact that he is God. Nevertheless, his power and goodness do accord with this stress on the necessity of moral judgement. As was shown in Simone Weil's remark about Christ dying before her eyes, the assertion of power can in itself make no moral or spiritual claim on us. So how does God's power fit into the scheme? During this century some Christian thinkers have in effect left considerations of God's power out of the picture altogether. Grossly simplifying a number of views, it might be said that in creating the world God took a great risk, for the only power he uses is that of suffering love. He makes himself vulnerable to the universe to the extent of being captive to it. The cross is the only instrument he uses for bringing us to our right minds, and the resurrection is to be seen primarily in terms of a new understanding of God brought about by the cross. This understanding of God makes a direct appeal to our moral and spiritual sense. But it has to be asked whether God was morally justified in creating the universe if the risk was so great; if we cannot be sure whether he will achieve his goal. If we are to put our full trust in God, must it not be in one who, when he brought vulnerable creatures into being in the first place, had some confidence that despite the terrible suffering we would endure he would finally bring about our ultimate fulfilment? There is then a *moral* argument against too much stress on the weakness of God.

It is also a fact of existence that every being has some form of power. It is not possible for anything, from an electron to an eagle, to exist without power in some form and degree – power being the capacity to have an effect on something else. What is true of finite creatures is no less true of God. His power includes an infinite inventiveness, so that through all the vicissitudes of the world God is ceaselessly and creatively at work, drawing some unique good out of each new evil and weaving it into the whole. But it is more than this. He has the ability to create *ex nihilo*; the ability to create out of the present universe a new heaven and a new earth; the ability to raise Jesus Christ from the dead.

Take, for example, the case of the resurrection. The resurrection of Jesus by itself, apart from the cross, has no moral claim upon us. But, given the cross, it is not simply an arbitrary assertion of power which we are free to ignore at will. It is a validation of the life, character and values of Jesus, an affirmation of his divine authority, and this is expressed in the way that is perfectly appropriate for God. It is God being God, and doing what only he can do: bringing life out of death. So although a recognition of the spiritual and moral claims of Jesus and the cross is paramount and indispensable, God's power cannot be left out of account. God creating the world and raising Jesus from the dead; God creating a new heaven and a new earth, is God doing what it is proper for God to do and what he cannot cease to do without ceasing to be God. That a person has, say, great musical ability is morally neutral in itself; but if he or she failed to use it or develop it in any way, that would be a moral failure. If someone as a result of genuine ability has been given power and responsibility at the head of a big international organization, but fails to exercise it, again there is a moral failure; a failure likely to lead to chaos and unnecessary suffering for others. God's power, we could say, is neutral in itself, but it belongs to him as God and as God he rightly exercises it as an expression of his perfect love, for our ultimate fulfilment.

God is God, and by his very nature he is our creator before he is our redeemer. It has been argued in this chapter that the recognition of God as the source and standard of all that we value is the only proper basis for his authority over us. It would appear that the assertion that God is our creator has in itself no moral force. Nevertheless, there is something else to be said. Imagine a home with a teenage son, in which there are endless rows about staying out late, untidiness, and general thoughtlessness. A friend of the family says to the parents, 'Your son doesn't feel appreciated; you ought to show him more love.' We accept this as a judgement worth considering, with some moral basis to it. We recognize that however irritating children may be and whatever feelings of hostility and anger they may arouse in parents, those parents still have a duty to show their children love. Although love must in some deep way be a free choice, based on the genuine appreciation of another person for his own sake, it can also be described as a duty. This duty is not something that is either chilly or arbitrary. For it is natural for parents to love their children, and underneath the irritation that is what most parents in fact do.

These reasons are pertinent also to our relationship with God. Unless and until we have cause to reject God on moral grounds, there is a prima facie duty to love him just because he is our creator and our God. Such love is natural to us. We have been created in the image of God, with a kind of homing instinct for him; and although this is not physical or psychological, but spiritual, it is no less real than the love parents naturally have for their children. So, to love God, beginning with an acceptance of his authority, is simply to orientate our being towards the light from which it springs and in which it grows; it is to allow our love to flow in the channel for which it was made. This point does not contradict the earlier emphasis on the necessity of a recognition of the supreme moral and spiritual worth of God as the only true basis for his authority. What it does suggest is the legitimacy of an initial, sympathetic receptivity to the possibility of God as God, of God as our God.

Authority implies and entails obedience. At the heart of Christian discipleship, for both individual Christians and the Church as a whole, is obedience to Christ. But the phrase 'obedience to Christ' can give an oversimplified and therefore false view of what is involved. It brings to mind the picture of someone giving orders and everyone else obeying them without question. Our relationship with God is not like that. There is much wrestling to discover whether what purports to be the will of God really is so. It has been said that the characteristic form of relationship with God for Jews is argument. Within the Bible itself the Book of Job is the classic example. Job refused to accept the conventional wisdom about suffering and insisted on taking the argument to God himself. Sometimes in Jewish humour, a humour which has helped Jews to live through their tragic history with courage and dignity, this argument with

God takes daring forms: in stories about Auchwitz, for example, in which a Rabbi and God dispute about who has gone too far, man in perpetrating such evil or God in allowing it to fall upon his people. Into our relationship to God we bring all that we honestly are and feel; and our ultimate response to him is achieved by way of struggle. It is very different from parade-ground concepts of obedience.

D.H. Lawrence, who was not a Christian, was at once attracted and repelled by the Christian faith. But he was a deeply religious man and some of his best writing is wrought out in relationship to Christian claims and values. In *The Rainbow* Ursula Brangwen tries to relate her Sunday world to her weekday world.

> 'Sell all thou hast, and give to the poor,' she heard on Sunday morning. That was plain enough, plain enough for Monday morning too. As she went down the hill to the station, going to school, she took the saying with her.
>
> 'Sell all thou hast, and give to the poor.'
>
> Did she want to do that? Did she want to sell her pearl-backed brush and mirror, her silver candlestick, her pendant, her lovely little necklace, and go dressed in drab like the Wherrys: the unlovely uncombed Wherrys, who were the 'poor' to her? She did not.
>
> She walked this Monday morning on the verge of misery. For she did want to do what was right. And she didn't want to do what the gospels said. She didn't want to be poor – really poor. The thought was a horror to her: to live like the Wherrys, so ugly, to be at the mercy of everybody.
>
> 'Sell that thou hast, and give to the poor.'
>
> One could not do it in real life. How dreary and hopeless it made her!
>
> Nor could one turn the other cheek. Theresa slapped Ursula on the face. Ursula, in a mood of Christian humility silently presented the other side of her face. Which Theresa, in exasperation at the challenge, also

hit. Whereupon Ursula, with boiling heart, went meekly away.

But anger, and deep, withering shame tortured her, so she was not easy till she had again quarrelled with Theresa and had almost shaken her sister's head off.

'That'll teach you,' she said, grimly.

And she went away, unchristian but clean.

There was something unclean and degrading, about this humble side of Christianity. Ursula suddenly revolted to the other extreme.[6]

Although this passage moves to what may appear an unchristian conclusion, it is worth considering for two reasons. First, it takes the teaching of Jesus seriously. It assumes that Jesus said things we ought actually to put into practice. There is no evasion. Secondly, Lawrence, through Ursula, is honest about his feelings. Most Christians probably share such feelings but have not the awareness or courage to recognize them properly. This inhibits them from grappling seriously with the problem of carrying out such astringent moral teaching. So most Christians either let the teaching slip in and out of their minds as something moving and beautiful, but which does not challenge them personally, or they seek ways of evading the question mark it raises over their own life-style. Lawrence, by facing the intuitive reaction of his being to the teaching of Jesus as it had been filtered down to him, struggled through to new insights. For example, he wrote two poems on the nature of humility, which begin with fierce denunciations of humility and end by affirming humility properly understood. Obedience, for a Christian, can involve this kind of wrestling for the truth; a wrestling for it before God and against God and with God.

It is also worth noticing that the model of divine command and human obedience is not the only model provided by the Bible for coming to right moral decision. The 1982 report *The Church and the Bomb: Nuclear Weapons and Christian Conscience* has a vaulable chapter entitled 'Wider theological and ethical considerations', in which Jesus is placed within the tradition of Jewish Wisdom literature. The authors of the report write in relation to this literature, found in the Old Testament in such books as Proverbs, Job and Ecclesiastes, that

> The two characteristic features are observations of the facts of nature and human life, and the quest for patterns in events. The purpose of the search for fact and patterns is not merely to acquire information. It is to learn from the consequences of the different types of conduct how one ought to behave. Wisdom, in the sense of understanding and respecting the given order of creation, and of living in harmony with it, is goodness; folly, which means in essence ignoring that order and arrogantly flouting it, is sin. Thus, in this way, through attention to the findings 'and warnings' of those who study the world, we can discern the will of God.[7]

Discerning the will of God is not just a matter of reading a rule book.

These qualifications, vital though they are, do not undermine the crucial importance of obedience to Christ. For most of Christian history it has been taken for granted that obedience is a virtue, indeed one of the main virtues. It was, with poverty and chastity, one of the vows taken by monks. All this seems strange to us. We have come to think that obedience can be a vice as much as a virtue. But it has an essential place in the Christian life. If many false forms of obedience have to be rejected, it is no less necessary to affirm the true.

Arbitrary fiats and peremptory commands, however confidently uttered by however powerful a body, whether human or divine, have no authority whatsoever. The sole ultimate authority is that of divine love: the heart and mind of God revealed in Christ. The only obedience that has moral justification springs from a recognition of this love, which elicits a freely given allegiance. On these terms, the acceptance of authority and obedience has an essential place in the life of the Church.

2 What is Revealed?

The Christian faith is not something that we have thought up for ourselves. It is, Christians believe, what God himself has revealed. It is because of this that Christianity is committed to some notion of authority. What divine love has revealed is authoritative for us. But what has been revealed?

We reveal something of ourselves in all our actions. A group of people arrive at a pub and one of them immediately offers to buy a round of drinks: he discloses the generous side of his nature. Sometimes the revelation of ourselves is closely bound up with words, with saying something. All priests and counsellors have had the experience of a distressed person telling something that has been on his mind and then immediately saying, 'I've never told that to anyone before.' In that intimate verbal disclosure something crucial about the speaker is revealed, and as a result the person to whom he is talking perhaps knows him better than anyone else in the world.

In our words and actions we reveal something of ourselves but not, even in a most intimate disclosure, all of ourselves. We come closer to that perhaps if we write an autobiography. A good example of this is *Part of a Journey*,[1] the journal kept by the novelist and reviewer Philip Toynbee for the last two years of his life. Although he did not, for reasons of space apart from anything else, reveal every aspect and detail of himself and his life, it is possible to say that he disclosed the heart of himself, the essence of who he was. The journal reads as an authentic, unillusioned, undeceived (so far as this is possible) attempt to respond to God through all the struggles of a difficult nature and temptations to carnal excess.

The Bible is also a kind of journal, though not of one man, but of a people; not over two years but over nearly two millennia. It is the record of a struggle to respond to the reality that kept breaking in upon them through all their deceits and failures. The difference between this and *Part of a Journey* is that it not only reveals the human struggle with God, it also reveals God's struggles with humans. It is true that *Part of a Journey* reveals something of God in addition to the central core of Philip Toynbee's life. It reveals something of God's purpose for Philip Toynbee. In the Bible, however, God is seeking to reveal something of his purpose for the whole of mankind, and it is this, just as much as the heart of humanity, that is disclosed. The key word in the Old Testament to describe what is taking place is 'covenant', or solemn binding agreement. For it is above all in promises that people reveal who they are. God promises eternal faithfulness to his people and asks of them in return a similar faithfulness.

The idea of a covenant comes to a focus in Christ. The generations of reaching out, of trying to break through, of endless forgiveness after endless betrayals, reach a climax in Jesus. Here, above all, God's faithfulness is shown. Here the very heart of God in unveiled. Yet, no less, the heart of man is disclosed. For the attempt of Israel to live as a faithful son also comes to its climax in Christ. He, the true son, embodies a true response. In him is the true covenant, God's faithfulness and man's faithful response. Here both God and man are revealed in the God-man Jesus Christ, not a hybrid but the true person at once fully God and fully man.

What is revealed is God himself and man himself. Since God is infinite there are infinite aspects of him which we do not realize, which could for all we know be disclosed in other creations. But in Jesus we have the very heart of God. Similarly there are many aspects of being human not even touched on in the life of Christ. But in him we have the very essence of man, his vocation to be a son of God.[2]

The crucial question about human life is whether there is, behind it, a divine power that can be trusted. Trust is fundamental to human life. Without an underlying trust that most people most of the time are telling the truth there can be no human communication or human community. Without a basic trust in their parents children do not develop and mature as they should. But can the experience of living itself be trusted, given the mixture of good fortune and bad fortune, happiness and sadness with which all human lives are woven? At the heart of the Old Testament is the faith that behind human existence is one who is utterly faithful. In order to make himself known to the world as a whole this faithful one calls the people of Israel into a special relationship with himself. He binds himself to them with a pledge of utter fidelity and asks of them, in turn, a response of total loyalty. Through all the betrayals, disobedience and disaster of Israel's history recorded in the Old Testament this remains the fundamental theme.

Jesus stood in this tradition and showed in his own person both the promise of God and the response of his people. He put his whole trust in one he called 'Abba, Father'. He responded with wholehearted obedience to the vocation he was given of proclaiming the long-awaited rule of God in human affairs; he lived with unswerving loyalty through rejection, betrayal, mocking and bitter death. He staked everything and gave his all. The cry of dereliction on the cross, 'My God, my God, why hast thou forsaken me?' expressed a sense of complete abandonment and let-down: there was no faithful one behind human life; if there was power it could not be trusted. But on the third day God raised Jesus from the dead: Jesus' attitude of total trust was vindicated. His life revealed that through all he had to endure there was, despite appearances, one who was utterly faithful. The promise of God is still there for us and will always be there whatever we have to go through.

If this is the heart of God's self-revelation in Christ, witnessed by the Bible, have the doctrines of the Church any point? If what really matters is trust in God, doctrines could be seen as a distracting and complicating clutter. But, on the contrary, they are essential. They exist to safeguard and to make possible this attitude of total trust. To take the most obvious example: the Apostle's creed says, 'I believe in the life everlasting.' This is not an arid formula, nor is it an optional extra to faith. It expresses one essential aspect of our trust in God: that he can be trusted even in and through the experience of death. St Paul said that nothing at all, neither life nor death, can separate us from the love of God revealed in Christ. In such a statement there is expressed the quintessence of faith. So the phrase in the creed, 'I believe in the life everlasting', simply makes explicit what is implicit in trusting God at all times, even in the face of death.

D.H. Lawrence once wrote, 'All that matters is to be at one with the living God.' If this is true, and if it is true that Christian doctrines exist to bring about and sustain that unity, a unity rooted in total trust, through every possible experience, how does this relate to the main articles of Christian faith?

First, Jesus is truly God and truly man. In the controversies of the first centuries the prime consideration for Athanasius, a redoubtable defender of orthodoxy, was what was necessary for our redemption. Only God can redeem us, that is, unite us to himself for ever, and therefore if we are going to be redeemed it is necessary that Christ indeed be 'of one substance with the father'. Similarly, as other early leaders of the Church stressed, if we are to be redeemed it is necessary that Jesus should have been of like nature to ourselves, with a mind and a will like ours, as well as a body.

Secondly, it is necessary from the point of view of our salvation that Jesus should have suffered the worst that can happen to any human being. That worst is not suffering or death but being cut off from the fount from whom our being flows. We don't experience this as the worst that can happen to us because of our lack of awareness of God. But Jesus, as the perfect Son of God, did. For him the worst possible experience was to be alienated from the Father to whom he had given himself completely. This did not happen in reality, but it must have felt to Jesus as though it had. He was condemned to death as a blasphemer, by crucifixion, which according to the Jewish law was a cursed form of death. In short, Jesus experienced hell. He went through the sensation of final rejection by the one to whom he was unswervingly loyal.

Thirdly, all that Jesus was and all that he went through is for our sake. He came to bring us into the same relationship with the Father that he himself eternally enjoys. Believers know, because they are joined to Christ through faith and baptism, that whatever hell they personally have to go through, whether in this life or the next one, Christ is with them, lifting them to the Father. As the Mattins of Holy Saturday in the Byzantine rite puts it:

> To earth hast thou come down, O Master, to save Adam, and not finding him on the earth, thou hast descended into hell, seeking him there. Uplifted on the Cross, thou hast uplifted with thyself all living men; and then descending beneath the earth thou raisest up all that lie buried there.

In Jesus there is a union of God and man, earth and heaven, which can never be broken. Through him, and as a result of him, we are taken up into that union. In the New Testament this union is that of Jesus with the Father, through the power of the Holy Spirit. The story of Jesus being baptized expresses in picture form the truth inherent in his whole ministry. There is Jesus himself, there is the Father who addresses him with the words 'This is my beloved Son', and there is the Holy Spirit, symbolized by the dove. Here is the Trinity revealed in human terms. This picture captures the essence of what it is to be redeemed; it is to be at one with the Father, through the power of the Holy Spirit. As a result of Christ, to whom we are mystically joined, this relationship with God, this union with God is ours, now and forever.

It can be seen from this brief sketch of New Testament faith that the denial of any one of a number of doctrines would fatally undermine a Christian confidence in God. To deny Christ's full divinity, or his true humanity; to deny his resurrection or continuing spiritual presence with us; to deny our mystical incorporation into him or the adequacy of his saving work to save us even from the depths of hell: these denials would remove the possibility of a God we can trust to the uttermost. Conversely, these doctrines or assertions about God are simply a spelling out of what it means for God to be a loving God.

The same question can be approached from the point of view of the problem of suffering. This, as almost everyone would agree, is the major obstacle to a belief in a loving God. The problem is so acute that it is only the Christian faith in its wholeness that enables a person to go on living in trust and hope. The Christian faith, considered from the point of view of its fundamentals, is a unity. Can we believe in a loving God without believing that this God, in his compassion for us, has so united himself to humanity that he knows our life from within? Can we believe that Christ was the very image of this God without believing that he was raised from the dead? For if Christ was not raised, his total trust in one he called 'Abba' was deluded; and if he was mistaken, is it possible to believe there is an 'abba' at all? A Christian priest was talking once with some Rabbis about belief in God. At one point in the conversation he said that without Jesus he did not think he would be able to believe in God. We could take that one step further and say that without the resurrection of Jesus it would not be possible to believe in a loving God at all. Obviously there are many millions of people, Jews, Muslims, Sikhs, and Christian Deists, for example, who do continue to believe in a loving God, even though they often actively disbelieve in the possibility of God incarnating himself in a human life. But when the full extent of the anguish of the world has been weighed, is this really a morally tenable position?

Since the Christian faith is a unity, it stands or falls as a whole. Pull one pillar away and the building collapses. A denial of one of the central doctrines of the faith cuts out the very possibility of there being a loving wisdom and almighty power behind the universe who can be trusted through thick and thin.

One nonconformist church I know has the following wording permanently on its noticeboard, 'On fundamentals, unity; on inessentials, liberty; in all things, charity'. It is a neat slogan but of course it begs the question. One man's fundamental is another man's inessential, and vice versa. There is another problem: is this statement itself one of the fundamentals or one of the inessentials? And anyway how do we know? The position taken here is that there are certain fundamentals and that the first and main criterion for distinguishing them from inessentials is that their denial constitutes a denial of the possibility of a loving God. It is possible, for example, for a Christian girl to refuse to wear a hat in church, or to insist on using artificial means of contraception, without thereby denying the very possibility of God. She may be wrong on one or both counts but her position is not self-contradictory. On the other hand a person who denies that there is life after death or that one day God will be 'all in all' is in fact denying that there is a loving God. For it would always be possible to think of a God who was more loving than one who created us just for a finite existence, and that was one who created us to share eternity with himself. Love has its own logic and this is the primary logic of Christian doctrine.

In his *Lectures on the Prophetical Office of the Church* Newman argued with great passion for the Anglican *Via Media* and drew a distinction between the central tenets of the faith as expressed in the Catholic Creeds and other items. He then attacked vigorously the Roman system of bringing all these items under the head of infallibility. His arguments are interesting. He believed, for example, that a legalistic moral system, covering every aspect of human life, takes away both from the mystery of God and the true character of faith. If everything is 'cut and dried' we lose the sense of the mystery of God, who is beyond all human systems; we tend to become complacent, thinking that if we do what is laid down by the system we have fulfilled our Christian duty; and we lose the chance to make our faith what it ought to be, a personal commitment. According to Newman some degree of uncertainty is essential in enabling faith to be a personal adventure and risk, something into which a person puts his whole being, in which he puts himself at stake. Against this it might be argued, by advocates of the system that Newman was attacking, that it is assuredly God's wish that we know his will, and as most of our life is concerned with minute particulars, it is his wish that we know his will in every detail. Furthermore, because he is God and cannot mislead us, he makes his will known to us with absolute certitude.

We have, in this dispute, as so often, a clash of different visions of God. If we here prefer one to the other it is because of the character of the teaching of Jesus in the New Testament. It is clear that Jesus, unlike the Scribes of the day, was not simply an interpreter of the Torah. In some instances he seemed to sweep away the scribal interpretation of the law and plunge straight to the heart of the matter as recorded in the Old Testament. He dug through to the basic principles as given under the old covenant. He also did two other things: he laid particular stress on the inner motivation or orientation of an action. Jewish teachers were of course aware of the importance of motivation and it is unfair to Judaism to pit a caricatured legalism of the Pharisees against the freer ethic of Jesus. Nevertheless, there is no doubt where the emphasis lay in the teaching of Jesus: on the thoughts of the heart. The other way in which he differed from his contemporaries was that he refused to limit the claim of love upon us. We are called to love our neighbour even if he is a Samaritan or an enemy. We are called to forgive to seventy times seven. There is a strong tendency in the human mind to want a tidy system of rights and duties, so that when we have done our duty we can relax and call it a day. The teaching of Jesus leaves no loophole for that attitude. The claims upon us are potentially unconditional. These three features taken together (the emphasis upon certain basic principles, upon motivation and upon the unlimited nature of the claim of love) cannot but raise a large question mark against any system of casuistry. It is true that Jesus taught us quite clearly about how we are to relate to our neighbour, but he did not do so in a series of detailed rules and regulations. Rather, he gave a series of stories, pictures and vignettes in which the kind of behaviour that might be asked of us was made clear.

This need not mean, nor should it mean, that the Church can do without a detailed system of guidance for its members. Jesus was born and brought up in such a system, and what he taught was not so much the abolition of the system as its subordination to something higher. After very few years the Church found that it needed to guide its members, and the sources it used for the teaching it gave were various. It used the basic principles of moral philosophy from the ancient world, accepted lists of virtues and duties from that world, some legislation from the Old Testament, the teaching of Jesus on specific points, and basic principles of Jesus applied to new situations and some of the sources. A glance at some of the ethical dilemmas of the modern world associated with AID, nuclear weapons, abortion, investment in South Africa, liberation movements in South America and so on, shows that in some respects we live in a different world from that of the time of Jesus and that if the Church is going to offer guidance to its members, it will not find guidance simply by extracting sayings of Jesus from the New Testament or verses from the Old Testament.

The church should indeed offer guidance to its members both on matters of personal and social morality; and some churches, not least the Anglican Church, need to develop a very different ethos from the one prevailing at the moment in order that such teaching can be recognized as having a real degree of authority. But this teaching cannot be regarded as infallible; and indeed the attempt to make it appear so only takes away from the proper degree of authority which can and should be accorded it. What has absolute authority for the Christian are the claims that come from the person of Jesus and his preaching of the kingdom. It is in the light of this that everything else has to be viewed. It is for this reason that the Church cannot claim infallibility for every aspect of its teaching, particularly its moral teaching. The consequence of this is that a distinction can be made and has to be made between the fundamentals of faith and other aspects of the Church's teaching. Some of this teaching needs to be taken a great deal more seriously by Christians than is at present the case, but it cannot claim infallibility.

Two other questions remain to be considered: first, the place of propositions in revelation. During this century, particularly in Protestant theology, there has been a reaction against the idea that God's revelation consists of certain doctrines. Instead, it has been asserted, rightly, that what God reveals is himself. He enters into, and calls us into an 'I/Thou' relationship with himself. This emphasis was a much needed corrective to the earlier propositional view of revelation, which tended to see God's self-disclosure in terms of bits of information about himself. God's revelation is inescapably personal. What God reveals is not words which we can stand over, manipulate and view in a detached manner. What God reveals is himself as our loving God and we know him only in so far as we know him as that. Unfortunately, this emphasis on the personal nature of revelation has led to a dismissal in some quarters, even in Roman Catholic ones, of the need for propositions at all. But we cannot develop a relationship with someone without coming to know something about them; and in all relationships, however intimate, it is possible, and sometimes necessary, to put into words certain things we believe about the other person. We put our trust in God because we believe he is trustworthy and if asked for grounds of our trust can say things about him. What we say, in short, is the creed, either the Apostles Creed or the Nicene Creed. The danger of having formulated beliefs is that these come to be seen apart from the relationship which they are there to define and maintain. The beliefs become objects to be manipulated at will. Though this danger is always there, doctrines are essential. They express and safeguard God's disclosure of himself as the faithful one who calls us into an eternal relationship of sonship with himself.

Some people find difficulty with saying the creeds not

simply because they are doubtful about some of the beliefs expressed there but because the mechanical recitation of these beliefs seems so different from their intimate personal prayers. They take their prayers as the touchstone of what our relationship to God should be like, close and highly personal, and a recital of the creeds seems by contrast impersonal and formal. But if the Credo or 'I believe' is taken not simply in the sense of 'I believe that the following items are true' but in the full Hebrew sense of 'I put my trust in', then saying the creed can become a profound act of personal devotion, as well as an act of identification with the faith of the Church. Saying the creed is in fact saying something like 'I put my trust in God, whom I believe to be utterly trustworthy, for he has shared our life to the full in Christ . . .' In reciting the creed, 'I believe in' and 'I believe that' go together in an act of trust which is at once profoundly personal, corporate and objective.

The other question concerns the development of doctrine. Newman in his famous essay on the development of doctrine wrote that 'To live is to change and to be perfect is to have changed often.'[3] This is true both for the individual and for the Church. In every age the Church faces new problems and it has to struggle to communicate its beliefs in terms that each particular age can understand. Each period in history has its own discovery, or rediscovery, of some aspect of the Gospel, or of some implication of the Gospel for personal life or society. This living, organic, developing structure of the Church raises the need for authoritative teaching in each age and for a body whose task it is to do this, a body whose authority is recognized by Christians. In short, this raises the question of the Magisterium, the authoritative teaching office of the Church. It also raises the question of distinguishing true developments from false ones. Here the only point that needs to be made is that we recognize in institutions developments which are congruous with their basic character, and others where there has been a change of identity. When, for example, a Grammar School goes comprehensive, or a boys' school takes in girls for the first time, it can still remain a school that is recognizably at one with the purposes for which it was founded. But if what was once a Primary School turns into a school for foreign students studying in this country, we see there a change in identity. The argument here is that Christianity has a recognizable self-identity; that certain developments are congruous with this, while others involve a change to a different character.

Much stress in recent years has been laid on the differences between cultures, between forms of Christianity in one age and another and between denominations. It is the perfectly proper work of historians and observers generally to explore all the nuances of these differences. Nevertheless, there remains something called main-stream Christianity which is not simply the lowest common denominator or a milk-and-water version of platitudes. C.S. Lewis, in the 1940s and 1950s, communicated a form of Christianity that was recognized as such by Christians of all denominations, and there are people today who are to some extent capable of doing this.

The Church is not static, and developing insights into its treasury of truth are one of the signs of life. For example, in the area of Christology there has been the recognition in this century of the true humanity of Christ, with all the implications of this: that Jesus was brought up and educated as a Jew of his time, that he shared an ignorance about some things, including the time of the coming of the Kingdom, and that he doubted and struggled as we do. All this increases our understanding and wonder that God became a human being like us. This is a development which is entirely congruous with the character of Christianity; it is recognizably one with what has gone before. But suppose it were asserted, in the context of a growing sympathy for the other religions of the world, that Christ was simply one revelation of God amongst others? Or suppose it were held that the affirmation that he is 'God of God, Light of Light, Very God of Very God' was a way of stating his supreme importance for Christians in the cultural world of the fourth century but that now it is open to the Church to assert his importance in a different way? Clearly, the first assertion could lead to a development of the Christian faith in which its self-identity would change. The second assertion is more problematical and there is scope for proper debate; but here too there is a high risk of Christianity changing its character into something else altogether.

In considering the question that underlies this chapter, 'What has God revealed?' it has been argued that God has revealed himself. This revelation inevitably involves certain propositions which express and preserve what is disclosed. There are some doctrinal statements that are essential. Those truths are defined as fundamental, and denial of them would in fact mean that God could not be trusted to the uttermost. As the Church is not static there is an inevitable development of doctrine, not in the sense of new doctrines appearing but of fresh or deeper insights into the faith once revealed. In deciding what is or is not a true line of development, a secondary criterion emerged for outlining these fundamental beliefs. Christianity has a recognizable self-identity and it would be possible for developments to take place in which it lost its identity. A distinction can and must be made between fundamental truths and the other teaching of the Church. This other teaching is authoritative but its authority cannot be of the same order as the essential saving truths of the Gospel. This is because the teaching and whole approach of Jesus calls into question all detailed moral legislation, even when such a moral system is necessary, as it was for Judaism and is for Christians.

Christian truth cannot be seen apart from our relationship to God; nevertheless it is false to think that Christianity can be free of propositions. There are certain essential doctrines which fill out the Christian faith that God is above all a God of love who can be trusted to the uttermost. God is Holy Trinity and as such is complete in himself. The Father eternally pours out his being to the Son who responds with perfect trust and obedience. The love which flows between them, filling them both, is the Holy Spirit. This love overflows, first to create the world and then to redeem it. In Christ God unites himself to human nature and takes us into the very heart of the Godhead, so that God is not only utterly transcendent, but we have been taken into God and God has come to dwell in us. This means that the life Jesus lived, which was a life directed to the Father, in the power of the Holy Spirit, a disclosure in human terms of the eternal life of the Trinity, is also our life. Incorporate in Christ we live towards the Father in the power of the Holy Spirit. These are the truths which, above all, are authoritative for Christians. They are not bare, abstract statements, but saving truths; truths which kindle our love for God and take us into a saving relationship with him. They enable us to trust him both now and in the hour of our death. As such they carry all the gentle but ultimate authority of divine love.

3 The Authority of the Bible

Whatever differences exist between Christians, all agree on the importance of attending to the Bible. Anthony Harvey has suggested that if a body accepts another writing as of equal authority with the Bible (he gives the examples of Christian Scientists and Mormans) it ceases to be Christian: 'It is only recognition of this story as its ultimate point of reference (that is, as "authoritative") which enables the church to continue as an identifiable society.'[1]

This agreed, there are still three major areas of questioning in relation to the Bible and authority. First, there are the Reformation and post-Reformation questions about the weight to be attached to the Bible in relation to the creeds, the formularies of different denominations, the councils of the undivided Church and the tradition of the Church as a whole. The sharpest focus of this questioning is in the relationship between the Bible and the *Magisterium* or teaching authority of the Roman Catholic Church. These questions were much on the mind of Newman and his friends, and although the area of common ground between the different churches has much enlarged since then, there is still an unresolved tension. This will be considered in chapter 5.

Secondly, there are the questions that arise as a result of critical scholarship of the Bible. The founders of the Oxford Movement were, on the whole, antagonistic towards the so-called 'higher criticism' of the Bible that had begun in Germany in the last decades of the eighteenth century. This hostility was one manifestation of their dislike of 'liberalism'. Later generations of Catholic Anglicans and

Roman Catholics since Vatican II have welcomed the historico-critical approach to the Bible and produced many leading biblical scholars. Though affirming the value of a critical approach to the Bible, those who stand within the catholic tradition also wish to affirm the community of faith of which the biblical writings are an expression.

Thirdly, there are questions about the relationship between the Bible and other 'great literature'. The last few years have seen a growing interest in this topic. For men like Coleridge and Matthew Arnold the authority of the Bible had to be related in some way to the authority they recognized in all important imaginative writing. For a hundred years or more our culture has been so specialized and compartmentalized that students of the Bible and students of other forms of literature have not been as aware of this relationship as their predecessors were. Newman himself wrote novels. More important, perhaps, he wrestled with the relationship between religious truth and imaginative truth.[2] Today there is a new awareness in some quarters of the interest and potential fruitfulness of the relationship between Christianity and literature. It may be that if a beginning is made on this third question the distinctive nature and authority of the biblical writings will be revealed in a fresh perspective.

A visitor from outer space reading the review pages of our 'quality' papers and major weeklies would receive the impression that novels, historical studies and, to a lesser extent, poetry, play an important part in the imaginative life of our culture. Every week, for example, new novels are reviewed. On the other hand, books on the Bible are rarely noticed and certainly do not receive comparable space. It is likely that this state of affairs accurately reflects the interests of most of the people who read these papers. The majority of the intelligentsia, we must conclude, have no deep interest in the Bible. Instead their outlook on life is shaped and nourished by works of art, music, painting, theatre and literature.

The Professor of English at Sussex University began a recent essay with the disclaimer that he wrote with some knowledge of literature 'together with a truly barbarous ignorance of the Bible . . . Such a state of affairs may well be thought to augur ill.'[3] In fact Professor Nuttall had some true and illuminating things to say about St John's Gospel, but it is the tone of the sentence 'Such a state of affairs may well be thought to augur ill' that is so remarkable: the confidence, the tongue-in-the-cheek bravado confirms that 'a truly barbarous ignorance of the Bible' is not, in our culture, thought of as a disqualification at all, even for writing an essay on 'Gospel Truth'.

What is interesting, if more disquieting, is that this state of affairs exists also among many Christians who happen to be members of the intelligentsia. It seems to be a fact of our time that many people, both believers and unbelievers, find their deepest source of moral insight and religious truth in the great European novels and poems of the past and in some contemporary imaginative writing. This is partly due to the fact that much of this literature itself relates to and reflects the great biblical themes. Dostoevsky, Tolstoy, William Golding and Patrick White spring to mind among the novelists. Among the poets Hopkins, Eliot and R.S. Thomas are just a few of the many. But there are other writers (George Eliot, Thomas Hardy and Samuel Beckett, to take a sample) who often grapple with Christian beliefs but leave the reader at the end with an unbiblical feeling for the world. Nevertheless, we read and admire such writers not just because of their talent or ability to entertain but also because we feel they take us deeper into the human experience. Christian believers, like others, are drawn to such writing not as a distraction but as a source of illumination and courage. John Drury brings this out well in his essay 'The Archbishop's Hat'.[4] The hat in question belonged to Richard Chenevix Trench. Its significance was that it hid a copy of *Middlemarch* that the archbishop was surreptitiously reading at an ecclesiastical function. Drury sees in this image a proper and fruitful tension between the believer and the agnostic. He is surely right. Believers as much as anyone else are drawn to such works, which reflect not only the complexity and ambiguity of human existence but also the moral strength and penetrating compassion of a person like George Eliot.

Study of the relationship between Christianity and literature is a re-opened vein that is already bringing much wealth. As George Steiner has written:

> Something fascinating is happening to literary criticism. Literary scholars, students of poetics, textual commentators and critics, are reverting openly to religious concerns . . . The currently fashionable analyses of 'narratology' – the ways in which literature tells stories, and the complex play of belief and unbelief to which this telling appeals – take the Bible for their working-model: witness the recent work of Frank Kermode . . . Once again, it is as if 'the Good Book' is being felt to be the archetype of 'good books' in general and of the complex means whereby our imaginations experience the life of the word.[5]

This interaction of the Bible with other forms of literature; of biblical criticism with literary criticism, is also bringing a new freshness to the reading of the Bible. Lord Eccles argued some years ago that although an agnostic he was yet drawn to the gospels, particularly the gospel of St John, as works of art. He could not understand why the churches had not made more use of this approach. In the essay already referred to, Professor Nuttall takes John 18: 33–8, the conversation of Jesus with Pilate and the judges, as a remarkably early specimen of what literary critics call discontinuous dialogue: 'the usual story told by scholars of drama is that the discontinuous dialogue in favour with the *epigoni* of Harold Pinter really began with Chekhov.' But in a fine contrast Nuttall brings out the distinctive character of John's dialogue:

> The world of Shakespeare's Gloucestershire scenes in *Henry IV* and Chekhov's *Cherry Orchard* is in a manner one place: a world of ill-disciplined servants, ill-managed material circumstances and asthenic yet poignant emotions. Here dialogue is above all desultory;

discontinuities occur not only between speeches but in the middle of speeches, showing that the characters are not only failing to communicate but as individuals lack coherent, autonomous drive. Madam Liubov's orchard, Justice Shallow's orchard; both are symbols of a sort of sweet-smelling death. But in the oblique answers of Jesus we sense rather an awful life.

The dialogue with Pilate may be discontinuous, then, but it is anything but desultory. We are not made to watch people drifting away from each other and themselves into a kind of reminiscent vacuum, but rather disputants locked in combat. The discontinuities of Jesus (and of Pilate – for he begins to learn the game) are evidently deliberate. They are at the very lowest a way of holding the initiative at all times. Answer a man directly and you are playing his game, dancing to his tune.[6]

The relationship between biblical and literary critics is a promising one. The question then arises whether the Bible could simply be offered as one book among others. People receive illumination where they find it; in novels, plays and poetry the human condition is flashed before us. The Bible could perhaps take its place with other works of art in the top league. But for the Christian this will not do. The Bible is in a unique position, for a reason which is as simple as it is obvious. God has taken flesh and blood at a particular time, at a particular place; God has become incarnate in Jesus. The Bible is our only record of this. What we discover there cannot be found anywhere else. It is not simply illumination about life but illumination from the light of Christ, the shaft of God's glory. This is in no way to deny the validity and importance to the archbishop and the rest of us of reading George Eliot; but it is to assert that the Bible has for Christians a controlling position that cannot be given to any other work. Not all Christians are cultured, indeed not all Christians are literate. For the *literati* there is sometimes a temptation either to approximate Christianity to what is regarded as acceptable to those the early nineteenth-century theologian Schleiermacher called 'cultured despisers', or to be apologetic about their faith. Both must be resisted. In the truths of the Bible, the intellectual and the peasant, the learned and the simple meet Christ on terms of absolute equality. He takes us as we are and asks of us the same obedience.

A further area of questioning concerns the relationship between modern critical scholarship and the authority of the Bible. These questions matter particularly to conservative evangelicals, but perhaps they should matter rather more to those who take the historico-critical method for granted. For there is a genuine dilemma here; it has to do with the difference between a devotional and a scholarly approach to the Bible. It is best imagined in an actual situation that commonly arises. Two ordinands go up to university to read theology, one from an evangelical background, the other from a church in the catholic tradition. Both are devout, both read their Bibles. Then for the first time they attend lectures and read books in which the text of the Bible is subjected to rigorous critical analysis. No question is too brash, no hypothesis about the origin and meaning of a particular passage is ruled out. The students are urged to be as critical and questioning as possible. Previously their reading of the Bible has been integrally linked with their Christian discipleship. They had read a passage in order to know the mind and will of Christ, and to know this in order to be obedient to it. Now, in the lecture room, the Bible is studied in a detached and impersonal manner, and both ordinands must adjust to the critical approach.

This transition is not peculiar to biblical studies. A girl studying music, for example, will have been drawn towards the subject in the first place by a liking for it, by an emotional response. She will have heard music that moved her. But studying the details of composition, for example, or the history of plainsong, though it may indeed have a large measure of intellectual excitement, will be done in a more detached manner; it will primarily involve the mind rather than the soul or the emotions. Similarly a man reading English who goes up to university having been much moved, say, by the novels of Thomas Hardy, finds that the detailed study of the texts is a much more precise, and sometimes dry, activity, compared with the strong emotion when he was just caught up in the novels at the age of seventeen. In all subjects, however strong the personal engagement, there is a necessary switch to analysis, comparison and criticism, in which the matter to be studied is treated as an object.

That this is entirely proper and necessary we can see in the case of a surgeon who is forced by circumstances to perform an operation on his own child. When performing the operation he does not love the child any less than when he is reading him a bedtime story, but he has to do what is needed clinically, as a matter of technical expertise, with the maximum of professional efficiency. When removing his child's appendix, he is not thinking about hugging him but of what has to be cut and sewn. He does not love the child any the less because he is treating his body as an impersonal object. In fact, just the opposite is true. Because he loves the child he seeks to perform the operation in the most detached, objective and skilled way possible.

So although there is a change in atmosphere from the church or bedroom when the Bible is read devotionally, the less hushed, more brutal atmosphere of the lecture room is, in itself, no sign of a lack of love of Christ. For the historico-critical method can be used with a variety of motives. One person may study the Bible and take a delight in debunking and shocking others. Another person might use the same methods while always running to the most conservative conclusions because of a fear of having his basic beliefs questioned. We are never in a position to judge what another person's motives are. I went once to Evensong in a village church in Wales. It was the eve of St Michael and All Angels. There was a visting preacher, who began by reading out the story about the fall of the angels in the Book of Revelation. He then put the Bible on the pulpit ledge, gave it a shove so that it slid along and hit the wall with a thwack and said, 'Well, I suppose you can believe that lot if you want to.' It seemed at the time mildly shocking, irreverent, and interesting. But whether the preacher's motives were better or worse than those of young men in red shirts on a beach mission, with black-bound copies of the Authorized Version tucked under their arms, only God knows. Both would claim to be motivated by a desire for the truth; and that of course is, and must be, the all-consuming passion of any serious student of the Bible.

This raises further questions, for every pursuit of the truth is based on certain presuppositions. The Western world is fond of its ideal of pure disinterested pursuit of the truth; and it is a noble ideal. But no study is value-free. Every form of scholarship brings to bear certain assumptions. There are presuppositions about miracles, for example, about whether miracles, however the word is defined, can or cannot happen. Our world assumes that on the whole they can't and don't. The world of the Bible assumed that they can and do.

Are there any indispensable presuppositions for a serious critical study of the Bible? Religious faith, or at least some sympathetic understanding of what it is to have faith, would seem to be necessary. It is fashionable to say that anyone, believer or atheist, can study theology and derive benefit from it. It is said that this is a subject like any other and that a person's own commitment, or lack of it, does not affect the validity of his work. Up to a point this is true. But only up to a point. A person with no feel for language could perhaps write an essay or two on W.H. Auden; but in the end he would be incapable of undertaking a serious study of his work. In a similar way a person without any sense of what it is to be a believer could hardly write a study of St Paul that got to the heart of the man. Karl Barth wrote: 'Theological work does not merely begin with prayer and is not merely accompanied by it; in its totality it is peculiar and characteristic of Theology that it can be performed only in the act of prayer'.[7] This approach does not involve a false or obvious piety, and it is no excuse for lack of rigour or critical acumen. But it affirms that the biblical writings were the expression of a believing, worshipping, praying, obeying community; and to understand those writings fully means entering into the same continuum of faith.

On a recent trip to South Africa I kept a diary, partly for my own benefit and partly for my family, who were not with me. At the end of each day I wrote several pages. I could have written about many subjects, African wild life or the goods in the shops or the physiognomy of the different racial groups. In fact I was mainly interested in whether apartheid was easing or becoming harder and in what the churches were doing in relation to this. This primary interest influenced the kind of people that I made appointments to see. My own presuppositions influenced the matter in another way. In order to get a true picture I saw not just white businessmen and farmers but people in the shanty towns, black priests and their congregations in the townships, novelists and others. What I experienced and remembered and wrote down related to these major concerns. But what I wrote was also for other people and it contained information about local birds and trees, special foods and other topics. These considerations, which I was particularly aware of when visiting a country for the first time, are an indication of how we experience reality. We cannot take in every aspect of everything all at once. We experience only what we are in touch with through our senses or minds, and what we receive depends on our personal concerns. What we remember of what we experience brings in other unconscious factors; and when we communicate it other factors make for selection of some memories rather than others.

All this, which applies to our personal experience, is notoriously true for historians. The past contains innumerable 'facts', but not all are available to us. Some, however, have become part of our corporate memory through being preserved in documents, diaries, the remains of buildings, and other evidence. How the historian selects and arranges these facts, what he judges to be interesting or important, will depend on his concerns; and these concerns will not just be private but will be related to the major preoccupations and presuppositions of his age. History, in Burkchardt's words 'is the record of what one age finds worthy of note in another'. So, inevitably, each age rewrites the history of the past from a slightly different perspective. History is a never-ending process: 'It is a continuous process of interaction between the historian and his facts, an unending dialogue between present and past.'[8]

What is true of our personal experience and of historians in general is no less true of the Bible and biblical scholarship. Biblical scholarship involves a number of different disciplines, linguistic and textual studies, for example. Modern scholarship on the gospels is particularly interested in studying the purpose, the presuppositions and general outlook of the writers. The four gospel writers wrote for different audiences; and they themselves had particular concerns. After the death and resurrection of Jesus, they told and retold his stories and sayings to various Christian audiences. No doubt they remembered and retold many things which are not recorded in the gospels. For what was remembered and subsequently retold or written down depended on what was judged important by those first Christians. As there were a number of different groups of Christians, so the gospels as we have them contain stories from a number of different sources. Each story in the gospels has a history. It has been shaped and reshaped by individuals and Christian communities who were in some way impressed by it. It related to their commitment and concerns; it spoke to their condition. Dr Packer, a well-known advocate of the inerrancy of scripture, is careful to point out that 'the assertion of inerrancy *does not bear directly on the task of exegesis*. Exegesis means drawing from each passage the meaning and message which it was conveying to its writer's own first readers. The assertion of inerrancy is not a short cut to determining what texts mean. We can do that only by studying the flow of thought to which each text belongs.'[9] This is an important warning, but does it go far enough? Each story and saying in the text has a history, and something of that history can often be seen. Biblical study involves tracing that history and seeing the story at various stages of its transmission and development. For it is related at every point to the Christian community which remembered and told it.

Recently the account of inspiration in evangelical circles associated with men like Dr Packer has been questioned. 'What is significant in the present context is that the standard line on inspiration has come under pressure from within the ranks of Evangelicals themselves.'[10] Abraham suggests that the old view, which works with the model of divine speaking or dictation, and which is associated with inerrancy, goes far beyond the biblical evidence; it is not the traditional evangelical view of the matter, and it is incompatible with the inescapable conclusions of modern critical study of the Bible. He himself suggests the model of a good teacher inspiring his pupils. This model allows us to speak of degrees of inspiration, for pupils vary in their ability and in the strength of their relationship to the teacher. It allows us to think of the abilities of the pupils being used to the full, for they are not passive, and hence the result will show differences in style and content; and there will be other sources of inspiration at work upon them and so it won't be a surprise if they make mistakes. According to Abraham,

> 'Inspiring', is a polymorphous concept. It is not something that an agent does independently of other specifiable activity. One inspires someone in, with, and through other acts that one performs. Compare at this juncture another polymorphous concept – farming. One farms by ploughing fields, driving tractors, milking cows, tending sheep, going to market, etc. Farming is not something one does over and above such activity; it is done through them. Similarly with inspiring. A good teacher inspires through his supervision, teaching, lecturing, discussing, publishing etc.[11]

It is not my purpose here to argue in favour of this particular model of inspiration rather than others. Every model has to be qualified and, suitably qualified, it may be that pictures of God speaking (thoroughly biblical) or God dictating (not so biblical) have a use. Every analogy is as untrue as it is true and studying theology involves suggesting where the respective areas of truth and untruth lie. The important fact is that there is an intelligent debate in conservative evangelical circles about the appropriateness or otherwise of particular models, which cannot help but bring them nearer other Christians engaged in the same task.

Whatever analogy is used to help us to understand how the Bible is in some sense divinely inspired, it is important to counteract the individualism inherent in most pictures of inspiration. The popular picture is of some lofty genuis writing in lonely isolation. But although some New Testament writers, most notably Paul in certain moods, and the author of the fourth gospel, were inspired in the way that we think of genuis being inspired, this is less significant than the fact that their lives and experience were grounded in the Christian fellowship. The writings of the New Testament arose out of the Christian community and were the product of the whole fellowship. Modern biblical scholarship accepts that the stories of the Gospel were remembered and retold many times before they took their final shape in the gospels, and then were written down in relation to the needs of the Church at that time. This theory helps us to see the earliest Christian documents in inseparable relationship with the Christian community. 'This approach invites us to see the New Testament, not in isolation, but rather as wholly interrelated with the on-going life of the Christian community and the Christian movement in human history – an on-going life which both preceded the NT writings and continued after them, and indeed is still developing today.'[12]

This means that when we read the New Testament we are above all put in touch with the faith of the early Christian community of which the biblical writers were members. Let us take a particular example, the familiar story of Christ stilling the storm, in Mark 4:35. Why was this story remembered and written down? It was not because Jesus performed something stunningly unusual. St Mark's gospel was probably written for Christians in Rome who were being persecuted. Working from hints provided by the Old Testament, where storms are seen as part of the forces of Chaos, and God's saved are precariously afloat in a boat, it is easy to see the import of the story for the first Christians. They were being harassed and persecuted; it seemed that their Lord did not care, that he was asleep. But no, it was their lack of faith that made them think this. Christ is Lord of the forces of destruction still, only have faith. 'The Lord is King, be the people never so unpatient: he sitteth between the cherubim, be the earth never so unquiet' (Psalm 99). To ask whether Jesus really stilled a storm on the Lake of Galilee, or whether it was the psychological effect of Jesus' calming presence; or to ask, if he did, what is the connection between his word and the calm, was it causal or coincidential, is to miss the point. The story is a mini-sermon that will have been preached many times before Mark wrote it down. Amid all the turbulence of this world, and our many fears, have faith: the Lord is King indeed. To read this simple and familiar story is above all to be put in touch with the faith, and the reassurance of faith over our natural human fears, of the early Christian community. So it is with all the stories in the gospels. They were written from faith to faith.

The desire to see in the gospel stories a straightforward, literal account of what actually happened or was said in the ministry of Jesus, however understandable, is misguided, for it is an attempt to picture Jesus without the faith of the first Christians in him. Every story, every line of the gospels, is written up in the light of the Easter faith, the faith that this man Jesus, once slain, had been raised by God; that his spirit lived in their midst and that he himself would return in glory to judge the living and the dead. Every part of the gospels is permeated with this faith; and the attempt to see in these stories only a literal account of what Jesus of Nazareth actually said and did is, in effect, a rebuttal of that faith. The first Christians remembered many of the things Jesus did and said, but they did not remember them as startling incidents in the life of an itinerant teacher. They recalled them as the human expression of one they believed to be the eternal Lord in their midst who was continuing among them the work he had begun in his earthly ministry. Critical Biblical scholarship, in making us aware of the slant or perspective of the earliest Christians in the telling and writing of their stories, far from undermining faith, in fact enhances it. For it puts us in touch with people who were incapable of seeing Jesus simply as a man; in touch with those who put their trust in him as Lord in the manifold crises that beset them.

The process whereby Jesus is seen through the eyes of faith comes to its climax in the fourth gospel. In Dostoevsky's novel *Crime and Punishment* Raskolnikov murders two old women. He is befriended by Sonia, a woman who has been forced into prostitution; and at one point in an intense, moving passage, Sonia reads to him the story of the raising of Lazarus. In particular she seems to dwell on the words, 'I am the Resurrection and the Life. He that believeth in me, though he were dead, yet shall he live. And whosoever liveth and believeth in me shall never die.' It is the beginning of Raskolnikov's redemption. The novel ends with him in Siberia, Sonia having followed him there, and the theme is resurrection to a new life. The book is about resurrection as a present experience, and it reflects the emphasis on resurrection of the Russian Orthodox Church. This novel, in its method and themes, is not totally dissimilar to the fourth gospel. That gospel too, in the story of the raising of Lazarus, is sharing the faith that Jesus can raise us from every form of sin and death.

When in the fourth gospel Jesus says, 'I am the resurrection and the life', this reflects the experience of the community of which the author was a member; the experience of being taken from darkness to light, from hate to love, of being raised from the death of sin to a new, eternal life. Which is the more reassuring for faith: to believe that Jesus of Nazareth actually said, 'I am the resurrection and the life', or to believe that the Christian communities which knew him after the resurrection as a living spiritual presence experienced the power of the resurrection to the extent that in meditating upon his earthly life they could only do justice to what they knew by picturing him in stories like the raising of Lazarus and in sayings like, 'I am the resurrection and the life'? My purpose here is not to argue for one or the other view, simply to suggest that the latter, in bringing us into touch with the profoundly felt faith of the first Christians in a risen Lord who was present with them, might be judged more helpful to our own faith than a strictly literalistic account of what happened. For such an account would only be the story of a man stripped of all faith in him as the eternal Son of God made man.

I suggested earlier that it is an illusion to imagine a study of the Bible free of all assumptions. We bring our presuppositions to bear, and what matters is to be aware of them. The predisposition that really matters is the one that comes from being a believing member of the Christian community seeking to be obedient to the Lord in prayer, worship and discipleship. This is the bias which enables a person to have a real feeling for the New Testament, for the New Testament is the inspired product of this community. As John Knox has written:

> It is true that we have the New Testament; but the New Testament is the creation of the community and brings us only the experience and thought of the community. To be sure, the New Testament has the unique value of giving us a kind of immediate access to the event as it originally occurred; but the event occurred only within the life of the primitive church and can be found only there. The New Testament gives us access to the event only because it makes us, in a real sense, participants in the experience of those to whom it was first occurring. As we read the New

> Testament, we become witnesses of the original event, not by getting 'back of' or 'beyond' the primitive community, but by getting more deeply into its life. For there is no access to the event except as it is remembered and embodied in the community.[13]

By reading the New Testament we get 'more deeply into the life' of the Christian community which stretches down the ages to the present, a community still characterized by prayer, breaking of bread and following Christ.

I mentioned earlier the problem of two students, both devout and Bible-reading, studying the Bible critically for the first time. In practice conservative evangelicals are more likely than those from a catholic background to be shaken by this aspect of a theological course. The reason for this is not simply that one group is likely to hold to belief in inerrancy. It is rather that a student from a catholic tradition will have his faith rooted in the eucharistic community. What he holds too, in human terms, is not first of all the Bible, but the worshipping community. This enables him to move in a less threatened way in the realm of critical biblical studies and also gives him more sympathy with the view of the Bible as arising out of and being related to the Christian community.

Two more points need to be made in relation to these students. First, the purpose of reading the Bible, for all Christians and churches, is to discern the will of the Lord and to act upon it. Study of the Bible may be an interesting intellectual exercise or a clever pastime. But what counts is discipleship: wrestling to know the will of God as he is both hidden and revealed in the pages of scripture. Secondly, biblical study, however critical and questioning, however confused in its findings, need not take us away from that aim. Modern biblical scholarship ensures that the will of God can no longer be understood in simplistic terms; it means that people might have to put a great deal more thought into discovering his will than they had previously allowed. A historico-critical study of the Bible usually results in an initial erosion of belief. As it progresses it often deepens faith. The Bible remains trustworthy, authoritative. For it brings us into touch with the earliest fellowship of Christian believers and their faith.

For the Christian, who believes that in Jesus, crucified, risen, ascended and glorified, there is the definitive disclosure of God, the Bible cannot be one book among others. He allows it to shape his thinking and acting; to mould his outlook and attitudes. He goes to George Eliot or Thomas Hardy or Beckett for insight. He goes to the Bible not just for insight but also for the mind of the Lord; and he does so seeking to be as responsive and available as possible. In the end we regard as authoritative something which makes a practical difference to our lives. Christian individuals and churches seek to have their lives shaped by the biblical revelation, in a way that they don't consciously seek to have them shaped by Jane Austen or Stendhal, however much benefit they might derive from such sources.

Earlier in the chapter I touched on the situation of the fashionable intelligentsia, 'the cultured despisers' of the Christian faith, for whom the Bible has not always been of any great interest or importance. I also considered the searching and unavoidable questions raised by a critical study of the Bible. Nevertheless, whoever we are, intelligent or stupid, learned or simple, the Bible exists for all of us to inspire and shape a Christian obedience to Christ. Furthermore, according to the New Testament the good news of God belongs first of all to the poor – those who have nothing and know they have nothing – neither money nor intellectual pretensions. Evelyn Waugh gets it right when, with characteristic irony, he makes Helena, the mother of Constantine, reflect on the coming of the wise men to worship Christ and then pray 'For His sake who did not reject your curious gifts, pray always for all the learned, the oblique, the delicate. Let them not be quite forgotten at the Throne of God when the simple come into their Kingdom.'[14]

4 The Authority of Conscience

Throughout history the claims of authority and the claims of conscience have been put into the arena against each other. Often it has been a fight to the death, the death of the one who acted according to his conscience; a death which has ensured that the flag of conscience will go on flying and the endless struggle will continue. This battle has taken place in almost every area of human life, most notably when the power of individual conscience has been pitted against the power of the state; and it is a struggle which has also happened within the Church.

In popular usage conscience refers to the feeling of unease we experience when we have done, or contemplate doing, something that is wrong. The emphasis is on what we feel, and the tendency is to equate conscience with bad conscience. When somebody says, 'I have a conscience about it', he means a bad conscience; he has a feeling of guilt. This emphasis goes back to the Greeks. 'It stabs with a goad and inflicts wounds that know no healing', said Philo, a Jew who was immersed in Greek culture. Some scholars argue that this is the primary meaning of the word in the New Testament. This popular usage is easily understandable in psychological terms. Freud suggested that we all have a super-ego, formed through a resolution of the oedipal situation, as a result of which we introject the values and attitudes that our parents stand for. This super-ego is made up of an ego-ideal, the kind of person we would like to be as a result of our identification with the people we have admired (in the first place our father or mother figure) and of an inner voice that says 'no' to us when we contemplate doing things that our parents would disapprove of. Whether or not the term super-ego is used it is clear that what Freud describes accords with what most people feel.

But if conscience is identified with the super-ego in this way the disadvantages are obvious. First, our feelings are a notoriously unreliable guide. Melanie Klein argued that our guilt feelings are related to the ease or difficulty with which we took in milk from our mother's breast. Frank Lake argued that such feelings have their origin in the birth experience or even before, in the womb. It does not matter for the present purpose which of these views contains most truth. The fact is that people vary greatly in the strength of their guilt feelings, and sometimes their guilt is irrational and obsessive. Secondly, our feelings of guilt will become associated with standards which may or may not bear any relationship to true values. A person might, for example, have been brought up to feel very guilty if he committed a social gaffe such as eating with the wrong knife or fork, while remaining indifferent to human cruelty.

It is necessary, therefore, to assert quite firmly that according to the Christian view conscience is not a feeling; it is, as St Thomas Aquinas said, the mind of man making moral judgements. In other words, it is first and foremost a rational activity. It is a person consciously deliberating about what is right or wrong in a particular instance and coming to a conclusion. This understanding of conscience is firmly built into the Anglican tradition. For example, Sanderson, one of the Caroline Divines, that group of theologians who pioneered a distinctively Anglican approach to moral questions at the end of the seventeenth century, defined conscience as 'a faculty or habit of the practical understanding by which the mind of man, by the use of reason or argument, applies the light which it has to particular moral actions'. Bishop Butler in the eighteenth century gave a famous definition of conscience which again stressed the rational element: 'There is a principle of reflection in men by which they distinguish between, approve and disapprove their own actions.' In Freudian terminology the conscience, according to Christian tradition, should be equated with the ego or consciousness, rather than the super-ego.

The rational element in the Christian understanding of conscience is the important one; but it can be balanced by affirming that conscience is an activity of a person in his wholeness trying to think what is right to believe or do. A person in his wholeness will include the feeling or intuitive element, and this is important. However much we use our minds it is still possible to deceive ourselves, to rationalize as right something which at another level of our being we know to be wrong. So our feelings, or our intuition, that is, God working through the whole of what we are, our unconscious as well as conscious mind, can be a corrective. It is always our mind that must decide, but sometimes when we are trying to rationalize as right a course of action that is wrong this other side will act as a check, leaving us feeling uneasy.

More important than intuitions from a Christian point of view is the spirit of God within us, purifying and illuminating the mind, so that we are led into the truth. This is a point particularly emphasized by the Franciscans, who have tended to think of conscience as uncreated light in the depth of the soul, rather than following the Dominican view of it as created light in man's reason. The Franciscan view has dangers. Some Christians have made a too easy identification of the promptings of their conscience with the leading of the Spirit. Christians believe that the Holy Spirit is necessary to purify and illuminate the mind in order that it may make right judgements. The question at issue is whether the Holy Spirit works in order to make us truly rational, or whether it leads us to do what the rational side of us after conscious reflection regards as mistaken and wrong. The former must be the true view. Given a choice between following what after long thought we honestly think is the right course of action, and obeying a voice inside us that seeks to suggest that, despite this, some other course of action is what the Holy Spirit is telling us to do, we must choose the former. The 'voice' must be listened to, and it must be allowed to question our often limited view of what is rational. The Holy Spirit is not irrational; it enlarges our vision and rearranges the priorities in our thinking.

The same point is true if we talk about Jesus Christ rather than the Holy Spirit. Bonhoeffer said 'Jesus Christ has become my conscience'. We know what he means. He was striving to achieve a wholehearted allegiance, an unswerving obedience to Jesus, the source and standard of all that is right or wrong. But there is no escaping the fact that it is each one of us who has to decide in each situation what it is that Jesus asks of us. That is the right thing to do; but in making up our mind what it is that Jesus asks of us it is we who have to read and think and choose, and this involves all our mental powers.

Newman's view of conscience could not have been higher; indeed, he argued that 'conscience is the voice of God'. According to him,

> Conscience is not a long-sighted selfishness, nor a desire to be consistent with oneself; but it is a messenger from Him, who, both in nature and in grace, speaks to us behind a veil, and teaches and rules us by his representatives. Conscience is the aboriginal Vicar of Christ, a prophet in its informations, a monarch in its peremptoriness, a priest in its blessings and anathemas, and even though the eternal priesthood throughout the Church could cease to be, in it the sacerdotal principle would remain and have a sway.

Newman was aware that few others shared this view of conscience: 'Words such as these are idle empty verbiage to the great world of philosophy now.' He was also aware that what many people called following their conscience in fact amounted to little more than self-deluded self-will. Perhaps also with his high moral sense, his ascetic life and his habitual striving to hear the word of God within him, together with his submission to the Church and its teachings, Newman was not aware enough of the gulf between himself and the vast majority of base human beings.

According to Newman conscience should not be thought of as 'a fancy or an opinion, but as a dutiful obedience to what claimed to be a divine voice, speaking within us'.[1]

Newman's view of conscience is powerful and moving: but these quotations taken in isolation from the rest of his teaching could be misleading. It is better to talk of hearing the voice of God *in and through conscience* rather than identifying conscience with the voice of God. Nor should conscience be thought of as a separate source of knowledge about God (a view that Quakers tend to with their doctrine of 'the inner light' but which Newman did not believe). Our knowledge of God is given in Christ. This knowledge is passed on by the Church. When we reflect prayerfully on what has been revealed, trying to believe and act rightly, we are acting according to conscience.

The Christian seeking to follow and obey Jesus, open to be cleansed and guided by the Holy Spirit, prayerfully *uses all his mind* to work out what he should believe or do. This is the Christian using his conscience. It is very different from the popular notion of conscience as the spasm of guilt when we have done something wrong. And whatever stress there may be on the importance of authority, rightly conceived, there is nothing, absolutely nothing, which can take away from any Christian the absolute duty of following his conscience in the sense defined above. In his various works Jean Paul Sartre sets forth the inescapable necessity and duty of each one of us to make up our own minds and take responsibility for our own beliefs and actions. This is inescapable. For, as Sartre suggests, if someone rings up and says that he is a messenger from God, it is we who have to decide whether we will accept this evaluation. Or, if we go to someone for advice, it is still we who have decided to go to one person rather than another, and the advice we receive will to some extent depend on that choice. Although choice is inescapable, we try to escape it. Through various devices, forms of what Sartre called *mauvais foi* or bad faith, we try to hide or escape responsibility. We might try to identify ourselves totally with our role. We might think of ourselves, for example, as a waiter, as nothing more than a waiter; we work out the role of waiter as defined by others, and thus seek to evade responsibility for shaping our own destiny and indeed our very self. But none of us can finally escape the burden of freedom of moral choice.

The Roman Catholic Church has often been charged with under-valuing conscience. This has sometimes been true. In 1832 Pope Gregory XVI wrote of 'the false and absurb maxim, or rather madness, that every individual should be given and guaranteed freedom of conscience, that most contagious of errors'. But this view was firmly repudiated by the Second Vatican Council and it is clear teaching in most Roman Catholic parishes today that even if a person is acting against the teaching of the church he must follow his conscience; that is, he must in the end do what he honestly believes to be right; and this is so even if what he proposes to do is objectively wrong. This was indeed the teaching of the Fourth Lateran Council: 'He who acts against his conscience loses his soul – even if he is in error.' It is the recovery of this truth, and the willingness to teach it, that has made it possible for so many Roman Catholic laypeople to practise artificial means of birth control and at the same time remain within the Church in good faith, including receiving Holy Communion and going to confession.

From what has already been said, it is clear that the charge of under-valuing conscience could never be brought with any justice against Newman. There is the famous statement: 'Certainly, if I am obliged to bring religion into after-dinner toasts (which indeed does not seem quite the thing) I shall drink to the Pope, if you please – still to conscience first, and to the Pope afterwards'.[2] If a person comes for advice on, say, the question of abortion and she is told firmly that abortion is a sin and that she must listen to the voice of the Church, yet she persists in deciding, after long and prayerful thought, that in his situation an abortion is the right course of action and the will of God, she must, however mistaken objectively, do what she thinks is right, that is, follow her conscience. For it would be worse if she followed the teaching of the Church honestly believing that it was wrong. It would be an act of deliberate wrongdoing and the Church could not counsel people to do that.

All Christians agree that we must do what is right according to our conscience. But we also have a clear duty to educate our conscience. This involves reading the Bible. A believing Christian, open to guidance of the Holy Spirit, can ponder the Bible and try to discover God's will for him. This will of course also involve prayer and worship.

Some of the results of this approach are disturbing. For a number of years Proctor and Gamble, the makers of detergents among other household goods, have used a logo depicting a man in the moon looking at thirteen stars, these stars symbolizing the original thirteen colonies of the USA. In recent years a number of Christians have come to see something sinister in this. The man in the moon, they say, looks like a ram's head, and this is one form Satan takes when he shows himself on earth. Furthermore, they assert, if you look closely at the logo you can see the number 666: and Revelation 13:18 says 'Let him that hath understanding count the number of the beast: For it is the number of a man; and his number is six hundred three-score and six.' The argument then goes that the Anti-Christ, when he comes, will require people to wear the number 666 in order to buy food and the other necessities of life. Such people will not be saved. In June 1982 Proctor and Gamble received 15,000 telephone calls on the subject, and some Christians started a campaign to boycott their products. Even granted that this publicity, however bizarre, might not be entirely unwelcome to the company, it highlights the fact that if the Bible is treated as a secret code-book the variety of interpretations possible is limitless.

This approach to the Bible cannot simply be dismissed as the harmless occupation of people on the margins of society. The interpretations that result sometimes have harmful consequences; and they are sometimes made by those in positions of authority, or in a position to influence those in authority. In 1982 President Reagan's Secretary of the Interior was James Watts, and among his responsibilities were National Parks questions. This is an important post, for there are millions of acres of land worthy of conservation. Inevitably there are clashes of interest between mining and timber companies and conservationists. Mr Watts is a 'born-again' Christian who believes that Jesus is going to return soon. His policy was to let the mining companies take priority. Posterity did not matter. When asked, 'But what would be left for our children?' he replied, 'We don't need to worry about that, Jesus is coming soon.' No doubt Mr Watts believed that his decision was a witness to Jesus and his return. To others it looks different. It would have looked different to St Paul too, who had the same problem to contend with. Certain Thessalonian Christians who believed that Jesus would return soon downed tools and gave up work. They also thought that considerations about the future did not matter in the light of the parousia. But equipped with his Bible and his conscience Mr Watts goes his own way.

There are even more important and potentially harmful issues than National Parks. Ed Macateer, one of the founding fathers of the Moral Majority in America, was interviewed on BBC Radio 4 on 23 August 1981. He said: 'We're living in the general age of the conflict called Armageddon in the Bible.' When asked whether the arms build-up might actually trigger off Armageddon he replied, 'Yes, I do, I positively even see that. But the Bible predicted there would be a day when men's flesh would melt from their bones and their eyeballs would melt out of their sockets. So when we relate that to what the Bible tells us, about ability for a third of the population, a billion and a half roughly, dying in a short day's period, then we can see how this Bible prophecy in our day is being fulfilled in the arms race, the build-up of that, certainly I believe precipitates that.' It is important to be clear why that statement is disturbing. It is not because of the defence of Reagan's policy, or the policy of nuclear deterrence. It is because it expresses a state of mind in which suffering on such a scale is not just expected, but almost welcomed, as a fulfilment of God's will for the world. When asked how representative his views were Mr Macateer replied, 'There would be up to a hundred million Americans of different religious persuasions that would agree with what I'm saying.' In other words a particular interpretation of the Bible is creating a climate of opinion in which the wholesale use of nuclear weapons is being almost predicted and made religiously acceptable.

Private conscience and an open Bible can result in dangerous social policies and attitudes. From the point of view of the Church the result of this partnership is no less disastrous. When visiting the small Welsh town where my grandfather lived most of his life I talked to someone who remembered him well who said, 'Of course, he was one of the leaders of the split'. In this phrase the pattern of Welsh village history, endlessly repeated over a period of about 100 years, was revealed. There was a dispute in the chapel and one group took themselves off to found another. There is a story about a Welshman who was shipwrecked on an island. Some years later a ship came by and sailed in to rescue him. The captain coming into shore noted two rather elaborate structures on the island. 'What are those?' he asked. 'They're my chapels,' was the reply. 'But why two?' 'Ah,' said our Welsh friend, 'that's the one I go to and that's the one I don't go to.' The tendency to sanction each quarrel within a church community with its own biblical interpretation and its own new sect is not confined to the Welsh. There are literally hundreds of different churches in the USA. Such a situation undermines the credibility of the Christian church as a whole.

This fissiparous tendency is a practical contradiction of the Christian Gospel. The ecumenical movement has gone a small way in reversing the splitting into smaller and smaller fragments. But there is, among liberal minds, an underlying tolerance and acceptance of the multiplicity of Christian Churches which needs to be questioned. First, the present Western valuation of liberty of conscience is, in terms of the history of the world, a very recent phenomenon. Even in England only a hundred years ago Jews and

Roman Catholics were barred from many posts, and Oxford and Cambridge Universities were closed shops for Anglicans. The recent appearance of freedom of conscience in the human sense does not make it any less important. On the contrary, like a flower which blooms for only one day once every few years it is especially precious, and we need to take steps to preserve what is of value in it.

Secondly, it is easy in the climate of opinion that prevails in the Western world to confuse genuine respect for the opinions of others with an indifference to everything. W.B. Yeats in his poem 'The Second Coming wrote that:

> The best lack all conviction, while the worst
> Are full of passionate intensity.

Christian respect for the conscience of others (so much in evidence in the guidance St Paul gives in his letters) is grounded in the respect which God in Christ accords us, which in turn reflects the freedom with which God has endowed us in creation. This is very different from the vague tolerance of a person who feels detached and ironical about every one else's view because he has no convictions of his own.

Thirdly, in a great many countries in the world liberty of conscience, which we take for granted, is not much in evidence. Furthermore, there are ominous signs that many countries in the world are moving into more authoritarian modes of government. In this situation it is crucial that the Church as a whole recovers its sense of a body under authority and with authority. Isolated individuals do defy the authority of an unjust government, and the source of their lonely courage is various, sometimes Jewish, sometimes Marxist, sometimes deeply held humanitarian ideals; and sometimes Christian. But dissidents are exceptional people. There are very few people in the world, for example, like Beyers Naudé who, after a long period of intellectual study and personal conversations with black congregations, came in Christian conscience to believe that apartheid is contrary to the Gospel and had the courage to break with the Broederbond and the White Dutch Reformed Church where he was a leading figure. He, like Bonhoeffer, is a person whose opposition is grounded in obedience to God's word in the scriptures. When Beyers Naudé was on trial for refusing to give evidence before the secret Schlebusch commission, he gave a moving testimony (using scriptural texts) that such secret methods are contrary to the clear teaching of the New Testament. He put forward, not just his own view, but what he conceived to be God's word, against the state. It was this which gave his stand particular force and authority. But men like Beyers Naudé or Solzhenitsyn are exceptional. Most of us, like J. Alfred Prufrock reflecting on John the Baptist think to ourselves that 'I'm no prophet' and kid ourselves that 'This is no great matter.' It is important therefore that the Church as a whole, not just individual Christians, recovers a sense of its God-given authority.

Something of what is possible has been seen in Poland. Poland has been in the hands of authoritarian regimes for many years, first the Nazis and then the Communists. In this trial the Church has been forced to develop a strong sense both of its independence and its divine authority. It is this that has enabled it to stand firm. The present Pope, nurtured in this struggle, is in fact the outstanding person he is because of such conflict; and his views on other matters (such as sex) also bear the imprint of this sense of the Church as a divine body with a distinctive message and morality. If the churches recover their sense of authority on political matters it is likely that they will also recover a sense of authority on sexual matters. I spoke once to a lady from Europe who had worked for a while with a church in South Africa. She had found there, she said, a spiritual reality very different from what she had experienced, as a believer of sorts, in the stale agnostic air of Europe. What had also surprised her, and made her think again, was the attitude to sexual matters. She was used to the free and easy sexual morals of Europe. In the Christian congregation to which she had become very attached, certain sexual standards were expected.

There has been a tendency in recent years to associate strict standards of sexual behaviour with right-wing, authoritarian groups, and a link has been suggested between sexual rigidity and political repression. This is dubious; but if true, it is only one possible relationship. It is likely that if a church recovers a sense of its divine authority in a struggle against an unjust political regime, this sense of authority will not be confined to its politico-social message. It is likely to embrace all its teaching, doctrinal and moral.

Although the Church teaches that everyone must act according to conscience, even if it means disobeying the teaching of the Church, it has also insisted that we have a clear duty to educate our conscience. This is necessary for the reasons already mentioned and also because of more general considerations. For we are all conditioned: far more than we are aware, the prevailing *zeitgeist* shapes our outlook. We all have a super-ego, or its equivalent; we all introject the outlook and values of our parents. These, in turn, will reflect the outlook and values of a wider society, both groups within it such as church or school, as well as the particular stamp of the age in which we live. If we took more note of the extent to which we are conditioned, we might take more steps to breathe the air of a different atmosphere, one in which we could breathe freely and deeply. At the very lowest, to try to educate our conscience, to widen and deepen our own point of view by the inherited wisdom of the Church, is a deliberate counter-conditioning, a conscious self-indoctrination in opposition to what has shaped us without our knowing it.

This chapter has brought to the fore the classical Catholic and Anglican understanding of conscience as a rational activity. This does not preclude the use of intuition; and the introjection of moral norms from our parents and the surrounding culture is inevitable. Nevertheless, 'following conscience' means deliberating, using our minds to the full, to work out what is the right course of action. For the Christian this process is inseparable from prayer and the disciplines of the Christian life, so much so that it may be, with Newman, that we come to think of conscience as the locus for hearing the voice of God within us. But this should in no way erode the concept of conscience as a deliberate rational activity.

Conscience is not an independent source of knowledge of God. This knowledge is revealed by God himself in Christ. Conscience seeks to be shaped or educated by this revelation. Nor is the Bible alone adequate for this educative process. It has been shown that complete dependency on the Bible can lead to a multiplicity of forms of Christian understanding. It is the catholic church, conscious of its apostolic authority, that has the educative role; and a Christian conscience will be aware of its duty to be so educated. For a Christian conscience is above all a Christian mind seeking to be responsive and obedient to what God has disclosed of himself. In our time the Church as a whole needs to recover something of this sense of being a body under authority and with authority. Unless the conscience is guided and shaped by what God has disclosed of himself we are likely to be carried along uncritically by the prevailing cultural mores.

5 The Authority of Tradition

Christians agree that the heart and mind of divine love have been revealed to us in Christ. But how do we know this Christ? Is it adequate simply to set an open Bible before a sincere conscience? The last two chapters indicated some of the difficulties of this approach. As Blake put it: 'Both read the Bible day and night, But thou read'st black where I read white.' This confusion appalled Newman. Few people have had a higher view of the Bible than he. Furthermore, he was as firm as the sternest Protestant in upholding the liberty of private judgement. What he wanted to ensure was that the voice of the Church, the Church in her corporate mind, was clearly heard. 'One chief cause of sects among us is, that the Church's voice is not heard clearly and forcibly; she does not exercise her own right of interpreting scripture; she does not arbitrate, decide, condemn.'[1] Bible reading is good and private judgement is a basic liberty; but 'Truth has a force which error cannot counterfeit; and the Church, speaking out that Truth, as committed to her, would cause a corresponding vibration in Holy Scripture, such as no other notes however loudly they sound, can draw from it.'[2]

The founders of the Oxford Movement did not believe that tradition provided an independent source of revelation. They did believe that tradition provided the eyes through which the Bible should be read. Why is it, asked Newman, that the Church followed the injunction of her Lord at the Last Supper about the breaking of bread, but did not make the feet washing a sacrament like Holy Communion? How is it that the Church has always kept Sunday as its Holy Day? Has baptized infants? The answer to such questions cannot be derived from scripture alone. The seed of an answer will be present in scripture, but the importance and meaning, and place in the life of the Church, of particular doctrines and customs depends on how they were assessed by the early Church. As Owen Chadwick has written about Keble's views:

> Therefore we may say (and Keble is not afraid of it, though he was much criticized for saying it) that in understanding the Bible it is indispensable to consider the tradition of the primitive Church. The Church not only puts the Bible before our minds. It puts the Bible in a certain light before our minds, and prepares our minds to penetrate into its truth. It arranges the doctrines of the Bible into a system as it delivers them, distinguishes the essentials from the inessentials, gives us help by its treasures of interpretation, and a mode of government and worship which forms the context in which the Scriptures are declared.[3]

To some people the idea of tradition is either dull or reactionary or, in the context of this subject, associated only with the post-Reformation controversy about scripture and tradition. This controversy will have to be considered; but it is necessary to set the whole concept of tradition in a wider light so that misconceptions can be dispelled. Tradition is not an optional extra. It is not mere decoration, though this may explain some particular traditions. The custom of raising a flag on special occasions or of prefects wearing a distinctive jacket could, no doubt, be easily dispensed with. But we are all members of a number of different communities, each with its own traditions; and some of these are vital to our identity as persons. A sign of the importance of tradition was the size of the audience for Alex Haley's *Roots* when it was shown on American television. Through this TV serial millions of black people reached out after their cultural heritage and identity. Since the Second World War nationalism, in one form or another, has been rampant. The Welsh, the Irish, the Basques, the Kurds, and the emerging countries of Africa are just some of the groups who have sought to assert their independence in order to preserve their identity. Sometimes this takes sinister forms, as it did with the Aryan policy of the Nazis and the modern emphasis on *Volk* in Africaanerdom.

But tradition in the sense of the religious and cultural heritage that shapes us cannot be underestimated. Hence the tradition of the Church, for a Christian, is not just a particular set of beliefs or way of doing things, it is the community to which he belongs, and the heritage with which he identifies; it is that which gives him his identity. The Christian looks first not to his *volk*, the people to which he belongs by language and ethnic origin, but to the *laos*, the people of God persisting through space and time. This is where he belongs, this is where the finds his self-image, and where he develops his self-hood.

Although the concept of tradition has a conservative aspect, for it is concerned with the past and wishes to conserve the best of it, its effect is often one of reformation and renewal. Tradition has a dynamic; it effects change. Almost every major intellectual change in Europe has come about as a result of an attempt to recover the past and recreate the present in its light. The Renaissance was an attempt to recreate the architecture and values of the Graeco-Roman world, the Reformation an attempt at reform in the light of the Bible. The founders of the Oxford Movement brought a fresh emphasis on the Church of the first centuries, and they were responsible for many new editions of the works of the early fathers, but this was not out of antiquarian interest. In this there was a difference between them and high churchmen of the old school, like Hawkins.

> His theory was conservative, preservative. Keble's theory is also in a manner, preservative – keep the deposit. But it is not only preservative. He had begun to compare the teaching and practice, common or popular in the present Church of England, with the

teaching or practice of antiquity, and to find the present Church wanting. Therefore the idea of primitive tradition is not only a preservative idea, but a quest for reform (Newman's 'second reformation').[4]

To value tradition is to be conscious of belonging to a living community with its roots deep in the past, but with those roots still sending sap to bring forth new branches, new blossom and new fruit. Tradition is much wider than the resolutions of Ecumenical councils or the statements of faith contained in the creeds, vital though these are. It includes the liturgy, the hymns, the poetry and the prayers of the Church as a whole. A Methodist when he analyses his sensibility as a Christian will be aware of how much he has been shaped by the Methodist tradition of hymn singing. An Anglican trying to spell out his identity as an Anglican will point as much to poets like George Herbert as to the thirty-nine articles; and within the 1662 prayer book he will be conscious not just of Cranmer but of the collects going back to the collections made by Popes in the fifth and sixth centuries. To value tradition is to know the past as a living presence. T.S. Eliot, at once the most tradition-conscious and most modern of poets wrote that tradition is not something we can take for granted:

> It cannot be inherited, and if you want it you must obtain it by great labour. It involves in the first place the historical sense, which we may call indispensable to anyone who would continue to be a poet beyond his twenty-fifth year; and the historical sense involves a perception, not only of the pastness of the past, but of its presence, the historical sense compels a man to write not only with his own generation in his bones, but with a feeling that the whole literature of Europe from Homer until today, and within it the whole literature of his own country, has a simultaneous

existence and composes a simultaneous order. This historical sense, which is a sense of the timeless as well as the temporal and of the timeless and the temporal together, is what makes a writer most acutely conscious of his place in time, of his own contemporaneity.[5]

A. M. Allchin brings out the force of tradition in his description of a visit to a Greek monastery where he spoke to the abbot.

One day the Abbot took me to see the monastery library. It was not a very large collection of books. There were a lot of elderly, well-used volumes of the Fathers. 'Here,' said the abbot, 'is a book which you give to beginners.' 'This is a work which is useful for someone who is depressed.' 'Here is a book which will give very clear instructions about the Jesus Prayer.' Any Westerner showing you round this collection of books, even someone to whom they were of practical use, would have said: 'Here is an interesting sixth-century text.' 'This writer shows influences from the Syrian tradition.' 'Here is a work important in the later development of Hesychasm.' We look at books chronologically and classify them in terms of influences and development. To the Abbot they all had a simultaneous existence and composed a simultaneous order. They were all books which were useful for life in the Spirit. Their authors were fathers and teachers who had become friends, to whom one spoke in church and at other times; it was of little importance whether they had lived six hundred, twelve hundred or fifty years ago. He showed me the library rather in the way in which an expert gardener might show you his collection of books on gardening, or a cook a collection of cookery books. These help you on your way. They are not an end in themselves.[6]

Within the Oxford Movement it was Newman himself who had the greatest feeling for tradition in this sense. As Professor Owen Chadwick puts it,

> This atmosphere is best expounded by Newman, because he possessed the most acute and sensitive mind among the leaders, and above all because he possessed by nature and by musical ear, and had developed by practice, a gift of writing haunting prose. He was incapable of representing tradition as an ecclesiastical device. It was sacramental of the life of heaven, the Church visible as a sign of the invisible. It was an earthly story of the communion of the saints in heaven. His feeling for historical continuity, his affection for the past, his reverence for an other-wordly sanctity, his love of 'orthodoxy' not as orthodoxy or rigidity but as faithfulness to every truth revealed, his sense of the richness and exuberance of the Christian tradition – all these enabled him to set forth the implications of tradition in magical prose.[7]

Within the tradition, understood in this profoundly Christian, believing way, there is the traditional tension between the authority of scripture and the authority of tradition, which even now cannot be quite forgotten. William Palmer, like the other members of the Oxford Movement, had no difficulty about affirming *sola scriptura* and in thinking that there was a clear difference in understanding between the place of tradition in Anglicanism and the place in Roman Catholicism: 'The difference between the Anglo-Catholic and the popular Romish doctrine of tradition is this: the former only admits tradition as confirmatory of the true meaning of Scripture, the latter asserts that it is also *supplementary* to Scripture, conveying doctrines which Scripture has omitted.'[8]

This view, even if it was ever true, certainly does not reflect the present-day understanding of the relationship. In recent years a distinguished group of theologians drawn from the Roman Catholic and Anglican Churches has met regularly to discuss the issues which divided them at the Reformation. This body, known as ARCIC, (Anglican Roman Catholic International Commission) said in its third report *Authority in the Church*: 'In both our traditions the appeal to scripture, to the creeds, to the Fathers, and to the definitions of the councils of the early Church is regarded as basic and normative,'[9] and a note calls attention to this emphasis in the Anglican tradition, in particular the Lambeth Conferences of 1948 and 1968. Neither that report nor the final one on authority write of any possible conflict between scripture and tradition. They are more concerned with the role of the contemporary teaching Church in interpreting both. Vatican 2 revealed some residual tension. Supporters of *scriptura et traditiones* fought against advocates of *scriptura sola* until the last moments before the final acceptance of the constitution, and this has left its mark on the text. For example, this sentence appears: 'The Church does not derive through scripture alone her certitude about all that has been revealed.' However, Bishop Butler comments: 'This statement does not affirm that scripture has a defective content, but that the cognitive process whereby the Church becomes certain of the full range of her faith is not a mere scrutiny of scripture but is a process to which tradition contributes.' 'This is almost exactly the position,' he continues, 'adopted by Newman in reply to the *Irenicon* of Pusey; Catholics do not say, he claims, that scripture is defective, but that tradition is needed for a discovery of the full contents and implications of scripture.'[10]

The *Constitution on Divine Revelation* of Vatican 2 stresses what chapters 3 and 4 of this book have maintained, that the Bible cannot be separated from the community of faith from which it came and for which it was written. It argues that before the New Testament was written there was a tradition of preaching and teaching. At several points within the New Testament readers are urged to stand fast to the tradition that was passed on to them. It was the Church which judged certain writings to be in the canon and others outside, and it was the Church, in its pondering on scripture, that was led by the Holy Spirit to interpret and preach its message. The document includes all this under the term 'tradition' and says: 'Hence there exists a close connection and communication between sacred tradition and sacred Scripture. For both of them, flowing from the same divine wellspring, in a certain way merge into a unity and tend toward the same end.'

Interestingly, Keble also used the image of two streams merging together.

> Because it is affirmed that the full tradition of Christianity existed before the Christian Scriptures, and so far independent of them, we are charged with alleging two distinct systems or words of God, the one written, the other unwritten, running as it were parallel to each other quite down to our own time. But this, by the terms of the case, is plainly unwarranted. If a man were to say that the Severn and the Wye rise separately in the same mountain, one higher up than the other, must he therefore maintain that they never meet before they reach the sea? Tradition and Scripture were at first two streams flowing down from the mountain of God, but their waters presently became blended, and it were but a vain and unpractical inquiry, to call upon every one who drinks of them to say, how much of the healing draught came from one course, and how much from the other. On account of those who would poison the stream, it is necessary from time to time to analyse it, and show that it contains no ingredients which were not to be found in one or other of the two fountains; and in so doing, it becomes incidentally manifest, at least in some measure, what portion each of the two has contributed to the general mass; it is manifest, for example that all necessary credenda, all truths essential to salvation, are contained in the Scripture itself; and is it not equally manifest, that many helps of greatest consequence, nay I will say generally necessary, to

> the right development and application of Scripture, are mostly if not entirely derivable from Tradition? And is it not a poor kind of reasoning to say, Tradition would have been worthless had we been left to it alone, therefore it cannot be of any value, now that Scripture has been all along at hand, to check, to sustain, to interpret, to rectify it, as the several occasions might require?[11]

These images of two streams flowing down the mountain-side and then coalescing, or two streams coming from the same well which meet and merge, are poetic; but they need some clarification.

> Sacred Tradition should not be distinguished from scripture as though they were two distinct realities, but only as a whole is distinguishable from one of its constituents. The relevant theological question is not: 'What does tradition give us that scripture does not contain?' but: 'What is the function of scripture within the total fact of tradition?' The word 'tradition' needs to be cleansed of its associations with an anti-Protestant polemic. It will then be seen to pose an issue which, as already suggested, is vital to Christianity: how is the unique history of Jesus Christ which, together with his person informing that history, is the fullness of divine revelation, is, in fact, the word of God made actual in historical event, made available to every man in every place and age; how is the particular 'universalized'? This is the question of sacramental actual presence – or rather of sacramental real action in human history. Scripture by itself can tell us about Jesus Christ; as inspired by the Holy Ghost, it can even, in its own appropriate way, put us into personal contact with Jesus Christ. But the witness alike of the Bible itself and of post-biblical Christian history seems to show that the Bible is not our only means of contact with the historical Christ. We find him also, or rather he finds us, in the

mystery of the body of Christ, that body which is at once the inner reality of the Church and her eucharistic focus and vital source. Within this total context of tradition, scripture has an important role. In all our personal relationships, while at the heart of them there is the fact that we 'know' the other, this personal knowledge does not exist without an element of 'knowing about' the other. Inspired scripture enables us to 'know about' Christ – about him whom we offer and who comes to us in the Eucharist, and who is the mystery at once in-dwelling, in some sense constituting, and transcending his body which is the Church.[12]

Like Bishop Butler, most Roman Catholic theologians today emphasize the unity of Bible and tradition. All is tradition, in the sense that the Gospel as a complete whole was handed over to the Apostles and is now handed down by the Church. (And the Church is part of the Gospel.) They would also emphasize that because tradition is essentially a passing-on it is forward-looking more than backward-looking.

Bishop Butler writes, 'Within this total context of tradition, scripture has an important role.' Does this go far enough? Scripture not only has its role of bringing the believer into touch with Christ, in its own appropriate way. It also has a unique function as a touchstone or litmus test of Christian teaching and practice. A possible analogy for the relationship between scripture and tradition is suggested by a selection for an art exhibition. The judges sit there as picture after picture comes before them. They judge some worthy of inclusion, others not up to standard. Then a masterpiece appears. At first they are doubtful about it. They are not sure whether it is a very good picture or a very bad one. Eventually they come to a consensus that it should be hung. In the ensuing weeks the picture gains critical favour. Rapidly it finds a place in the canon of great English painting. That picture, once itself judged, becomes a standard for other works. This was, in fact, true though unrecognized when it was first submitted. The judges were evaluating it, but in a profound sense it was their critical sense that was judged. They were being asked as it were, to recognize the intrinsic worth of a picture which though it was part of the tradition of English painting would in fact call that tradition into question and shape its future course.

So it was that the Church, over a period of about two hundred years, agreed that certain writings should be in, and others out, of what came to be called the canon of the New Testament. That act of recognition once made, the Bible then came to have, and rightly to have, an authority independent of the tradition of which it was a part and which made it what it was. The Bible, as Bishop Butler suggests, is best seen as part of the whole tradition. But it has a unique role within that tradition, as our only early written record, to guide us on what is and what is not crucial to the Church's identity. It has a unique, controlling, final court-of-appeal type of authority. When Augustine was arguing with the Arians and both were in the position of appealing to councils that the other did not regard as a true council of the Church, Augustine said, 'Let the issue be debated point for point, cause for cause, and reason for reason on the authority of the scriptures, which are not peculiar to either but common to both.'

Newman and his friends would have agreed wholeheartedly with Augustine: but in interpreting the Bible they also appealed to Augustine and the other early fathers. They appealed to tradition; they held it to be authoritative, as giving us a sure, apostolic guide to the reading of scripture. Newman wrote, 'Whatever doctrine the primitive ages unanimously attest, whether by consent of the Fathers, or by Councils, or by the events of history, or by controversies, or in whatever way, whatever may fairly and reasonably be considered to be the universal belief of those ages, is to be received as coming from the Apostles. . . . Catholicity, Antiquity, and consent of the Fathers, is the proper evidence of the fidelity or apostolicity of a professed Tradition.'[13] They appealed to the Vincentian Canon, the famous statement of St Vincentius of Lerins, *Quod semper, quod ubique, quod ab omnibus,* what has been taught always, everywhere, by all.

Newman sharply distinguished his interest in tradition from antiquarianism. He was not concerned with 'incense and oil, insufflations and stoles with crosses on them'. Nor was he presuming to judge what any particular Christian had to believe if he was to be saved. Only God could do that, and while he might save a labourer on the basis of a rudimentary faith he might ask a great deal more of a theologian. Newman was concerned with the corporate judgement of the Church on what it should teach in the name of Christ: 'Our purpose is to determine merely this – what doctrine the Church Catholic will *teach* indefectibly, what doctrines she must *enforce* as a condition of communion, what doctrines she must rescue from a scrutiny of Private Judgement; in a word, what doctrines are the foundation of the Church.'[14]

The Bible has a unique authority. It is at once the product of the community of faith and the source and standard. All Christians today look to it as a final court of appeal on what is authetically Christian. Nevertheless, the effect of the Bible varies greatly depending on the cultural milieu in which it is studied. The Bible as interpreted by the followers of Ouspensky, or spiritualists, or exponents of the perennial philosophy is very different from the Bible as read by New Testament scholars. Until a few years ago the Bible as preached and taught in conservative evangelical circles had a very different 'feel' about it from the way it was expounded in Roman Catholic churches. This went beyond the interpretation of particular texts; it had to do with the whole sense and grasp of what Christian faith is about. As a particular biblical scene like the nativity has been painted in multiple ways down the ages, reflecting not just the style but the whole outlook of particular schools of painting, so the Bible has been seen differently by different cultures and has shaped their vision. The way the Church of the first centuries felt about its faith, the way it interpreted the Bible as a whole, has a uniquely helpful role among the different traditions. The early Church may have developed practices or beliefs which subsequent generations of Christians were right to question. But to suggest that the Church of the first five centuries was mistaken in affirming Christ to be 'Very God of Very God', as well as fully and properly human, would suggest making Christianity something else altogether.

The Christian faith is all of a piece. There are certain central pillars: if one is pulled out, the whole building collapses. People are free to deny the Christian faith or to interpret it in any way that in conscience they feel they must do. But the Christian faith, historically understood, has a wholeness about it, an internal coherence and consistency. As William Palmer put it, 'The authenticity of primitive tradition and its records, of Scripture and its doctrines, and of Christianity as a revelation, stand or fall together.'[15]

This chapter has tried to show that tradition is not something of merely antiquarian interest. Tradition is vital to our self-identity and, properly understood, is the source of renewal, not stagnation. Christians belong to a tradition which shapes their self-understanding and gives them identity. At the heart of this tradition is God's revelation of himself in Christ, knowledge of which the Church passes on from generation to generation. Bible and tradition should not be set against each other, for the Bible is part of the one continuum of Christian life stretching back to the Apostles. Nevertheless, the Bible has a unique controlling function in keeping the tradition true to its origin and in ensuring that it retains its identity. Furthermore, although questioning and scholarship will never cease it is right that there should be a basic trust, which is nothing less than a trust in the promise that the Holy Spirit will lead the Church into all truth, that the early Church faithfully interpreted the mind of Christ.

God has revealed himself in Christ. The Christian recognizes in this the supreme self-disclosure of divine love. For this reason, and on this basis, this revelation has ultimate authority. This leads the Christian mind, both individually and as part of the Church as a whole, to be responsive, to be obedient to the disclosure. The quest leads him to the Bible and then, for reasons discussed, to the tradition of the Church; in particular to the decisions of the Ecumenical councils of the undivided Church and the creeds. But what weight can be attached to these affirmations of faith? Can they be regarded as infallible?

6 Infallibility and the Mind of the Faithful

Few have been as critical of the notion of infallibility as Newman in his Anglican days. In *Lectures on the Prophetical Office of the Church viewed relatively to Romanism and Popular Protestantism*, published in 1837, he argued that if you appeal to antiquity the notion of infallibility can be shown to be a late development. Further, he argued, it is morally defective, preventing a true grasp of the faith, which always involves personal venture and personal commitment in relation to what is not known with certitude; and it is politically dangerous. Newman appealed to antiquity because he believed that the teaching of the Church on essential points of doctrine could be clearly seen there. A doctrine of infallibility was not needed because if people looked to the first centuries they could see the firm outlines of Christian doctrine. An allegedly infallible Church could neither add to nor subtract from that. Infallibility could not confer any more authority on this body of teaching than it already had, and private opinion could not alter what was there.

This body of essential doctrine could be labelled apostolic, and the Church had a duty to conserve and communicate it from generation to generation. In this task it would be guided by the Holy Spirit: 'Not only is the Church Catholic bound to teach the Truth, but she is ever divinely guided to teach it; her witness of the Christian faith is a matter of promise as well as of duty; her discernment of it is secured by a heavenly as well as a human rule. She is indefectible in it, and therefore not only has authority to enforce, but is of authority in declaring it'?[1] But it is in the essentials of the faith, not in every detail, that the Church is indefectible: 'We Anglicans say, that the Church Catholic will ever retain what is called in Scripture "the faith", the substance or great outlines of the Gospel as taught by the Apostles (whatever they are, which is not the question at present), and that in consequence of the Scripture promise that the word of God shall never depart out of her mouth. Romanists say that she is pure and spotless in all matters great and small, that she can never decide wrongly on any point of faith and morals, but in every age possesses and teaches explicitly or implicitly the whole truth.'[2]

The Anglican Church, however, appealed to the undivided Church for her witness to the essentials. 'That original Creed, which St Paul committed to Timothy, and the first ages considered as the fundamental faith, still remains to us, and to all Christians all over the world; the gates of hell have not prevailed against it . . . still we have the essentials of faith: and that we have as much as this, considering the numberless hazards to which it has been exposed, is at once a most gracious and most marvellous appointment of Divine Providence.'[3]

Newman writes further:

> Whether we be right or wrong, our theory of religion has a meaning, and that really distinct from Romanism. Both we and Romanists hold that the Church Catholic is unerring in its declarations of faith, or saving doctrine; but we differ from each other as to what is the faith, and the Church Catholic . . . they understand by the Faith, whatever the Church at any time declares to be faith; we what it has actually so declared from the beginning. We hold that the Church Catholic will never depart from those outlines of doctrine which the Apostles formally published; they that she will never depart in any of her acts from that entire system, written and oral, public and private, explicit and implicit, which they received and taught; we that she has a gift of fidelity, they of

> discrimination . . . The creed of Romanism is ever subject to increase; ours is fixed once for all.'[4]

'Ours is fixed once for all', wrote the Anglican Newman. Yet each age brings a new configuration of social and political circumstances which profoundly affects our understanding of the Gospel and response to it. An aspect of the faith which may be present in the Bible, but which is not emphasized, has its implications drawn out and its importance stressed in some subsequent generation. For example, the doctrine of purgatory was developed in the eleventh century and became crucial to the whole of Christendom for five centuries. Belief in purgatory can be grounded in St Paul's teaching, but it is not an aspect of the faith that is central to his writings. In the Middle Ages this doctrine was developed; the acorn became a great oak. How do we distinguish a true development from a false one?

The Church, seeking the mind of Christ in order to be obedient to it, turns to primitive tradition. This by itself, however, is not enough. For the Church is an organic, living body, with fresh decisions to make. Each age brings new circumstances. New problems arise and lead Christians in every generation to draw further insights from the Bible and the tradition as a whole. They develop the implications of aspects of the past in order to meet contemporary needs. Some people feel, without giving the matter much thought, that a development of the Christian faith is bound to mean a corruption of the faith. As a Roman Catholic, Newman came to challenge this instinctive antipathy to the idea of development:

> It is indeed sometimes said that the stream is clearest near the spring. Whatever use may fairly be made of this image, it does not apply to the history of a philosophy or sect, which, on the contrary, is more equable, and purer, and stronger, when its bed has become deep, and broad, and full. It necessarily rises out of an existing state of things, and, for a time, savours of the soil. Its vital element needs disengaging

from what is foreign and temporary, and is employed in efforts after freedom, more vigorous and hopeful as its years increase. Its beginnings are no measure of its capabilities, nor of its scope. At first, no one knows what it is, or what it is worth. It remains perhaps for a time quiescent: it tries, as it were, its limbs, and proves the ground under it, and feels its ways. From time to time, it makes essays which fail, and are in consequence abandoned. It seems in suspense which way to go; it wavers, and at length strikes out in one definite direction. In time it enters upon strange territory; points of controversy alter their bearing; parties rise and fall about it; dangers and hopes appear in new relations, and old principles reappear under new forms; it changes with them in order to remain the same. In a higher world it is otherwise; but here below to live is to change, and to be perfect is to have changed often.[5]

In the famous essay from which that quotation came Newman outlined criteria for distinguishing true from false development. One of the tests, for example, is whether the original idea is genuinely preserved: 'A true development, then, may be described as one which is conservative of the course of development which went before it, which is that development and something besides: it is an addition which illustrates, not obscures, corroborates, not corrects, the body of thought from which it proceeds; and this is its characteristic as contrasted with a corruption.'[6]

Newman's views on development have been widely accepted in the Roman Catholic Church. The *Constitution on Divine Revelation* of Vatican 2 said:

This tradition which comes from the apostles develops in the Church with the help of the Holy Spirit. For there is a growth in the understanding of the realities and the words which have been handed down. This happens through the contemplation and study made by believers, who treasure these things in their hearts

> (cf. Luke 2:29, 51), through the intimate study of spiritual things they experience, and through the preaching of those who have received through episcopal succession the sure gift of truth. For, as the centuries succeed one another, the Church constantly moves forward toward the fullness of divine truth until the words of God reach their complete fulfilment in her.[7]

Bishop Butler, commenting on this passage, wrote that it 'is practically a précis of Newman's theory of the development of doctrine'.[8]

'To live is to change.' In each generation the Church has had to make decisions. How far is it possible to speak of these decisions as infallible? Infallibility is a negative concept meaning 'kept from error'. 'In Roman Catholic doctrine, infallibility means only the preservation of the judgement from error for the maintenance of the Church in the truth, not positive inspiration or revelation.'[9]

The idea of infallibility has been the subject of such polemic, from the Orthodox, from Protestants and, not least, from within the Roman Catholic Church itself, that it is impossible to discuss the subject calmly and judiciously without two reminders. First, the notion does not in the first place belong to the papacy. Any discussion that begins from the assertion or denial of papal infallibility is doomed to cause deep division from the outset. Infallibility, if it has a place in Christian thinking, belongs first to the Church as a whole, secondly to the teaching office of the Church (the Magisterium), and only thirdly to the papacy.

Secondly, it is impossible to get to the heart of the discussion without an awareness of the fundamentally religious motivation and genuinely spiritual passion behind the idea. This may sound obvious or patronizing, but one result of so much acrimonious controversy is that it is often neglected. The spiritual roots of infallibility lie in the conviction of the first Christians that through his spirit the risen, ascended and glorified Christ remained with them and that this spirit would lead them into all truth. As Kung has written,

> It is clear that the promises given to the Church must be acknowledged. No believing Christian who bases himself on the New Testament can dispute this. We need only recall the scriptural texts constantly quoted in this connection: Matthew 16:18, 'The gates of the underworld can never hold out against it'; Matthew 28:20, 'And know that I am with you always; yes to the end of time'; John 14:16, 'And he (the Father) will give you another Advocate to be with you for ever, the Spirit of truth'; John 16:13, 'The Spirit . . . will lead you to the complete truth'; Timothy 3:15, 'The Church of the living God, which upholds the truth and keeps it safe'.[10]

The same idea may be approached from the Christian belief in divine providence. A Christian reflecting on his own experience knows that he is a believer, or that he has a particular vocation, only because God's grace has gone before and worked in his life. Without falling into the simplistic view that everything that happens is for the best, he nevertheless believes in faith that his life has been and will continue to be in the hands of God. What is true at an individual level is no less true in relation to the Church as a whole. When a Christian reflects on the long history of the Church from New Testament times to the present day, with all its weaknesses, faults and errors, it is still necessary to affirm that this history has been in the hands of God, and that God has preserved it from fundamental error; for this, if for no other reason, that I who now believe, believe only through the community of Christians down the ages which has faithfully transmitted to me the Gospel. Even now as I lift my heart in prayer to the Father, through the Son, in the power of the Holy Spirit within me, I witness to the profound sense in which God has preserved his Church from error. For my faith is not my individual possession. It is a sharing in the faith of the Church or, even more mysteriously, a sharing in the faith of Christ himself who dwells in his Church. As Geoffrey Wainwright, a Methodist, put it: 'On several occasions already we have needed to say that the Christian vision supposes at least a minimal belief in God's providential guidance of the Church. This was the case with the composition of the scriptures and the establishment and definition of the scriptural canon. . . . All Christian worship explicitly or implicitly invokes the Holy Spirit who, according to the Johannine Christ, will lead believers into all the truth.'[11]

The conviction of the first Christians that Christ remains with his Church, and even a minimal understanding of divine providence, both suggest an initial sympathy for the idea that God has kept, and will keep, his Church from error in matters of saving truth. But what is meant by the Church in this context? Not, it must be stressed, the bishops and Pope in isolation but the whole body of the faithful. The *Dogmatic Constitution on the Church* of the Second Vatican Council affirms this: 'The body of the faithful as a whole, anointed as they are by the Holy One (cf. John 2:20, 27), cannot err in matters of belief. Thanks to a supernatural sense of the faith which characterizes the people as a whole, it manifests this unerring quality when, "from the bishops down to the last members of the laity," it shows universal agreement in matters of faith and morals.' This passage fills out the meaning of the Latin phrase, *sensus fidelium*, which I have translated as 'the mind of the faithful'. The idea of a *sensus fidelium* was a favourite theme of Cardinal Newman.[12] It was fully affirmed at Vatican 2, with the result that 'the church conducts her doctrinal and theological reflections within a collective and collaborative climate of opinion'.[13]

Yves Congar in an exhaustive study of the concept of infallibility in the Middle Ages wrote:

> The universally shared basic belief was that the *Ecclesia* herself could not err . . . By Ecclesia is understood the Church in her totality, as *congregatio* or *universitas fidelium*. One part or another of the Church could

> err, and even the bishops or the Pope could; the Church could be storm-tossed, but in the end she remained faithful . . . It was generally assumed that the Pope could err and fall into heresy . . . A pope who fell into heresy *ipso facto* ceased to be head of the Church, because he had ceased to be a member of it.[14]

Although there is some stress in Orthodox theology on the infallibility of the ecumenical councils, this may have been a reaction to Roman Catholic claims on behalf of the papacy. A more representative Orthodox position is that which emphasizes the Church as a whole. In 1848 the Orthodox Patriarchs wrote to Pius IX (without however deterring him from promulgating either the definition of the Immaculate Conception or that of his own infallibility): 'Among us neither patriarchs nor councils could ever introduce new teaching, for the guardian of religion is the very body of the Church, that is, the people (laos) itself.'[15]

An important Russian theologian, Alexei Khomiakov, commenting on these exchanges at the time, wrote: 'The Pope is greatly mistaken in supposing that we consider the ecclesiastical hierarchy to be the guardian of dogma. The case is quite different. The unvarying constancy and the unerring truth of Christian dogma does not depend on any hierarchical order; it is guarded by the totality, by the whole people of the Church, which is the Body of Christ.'[16]

This teaching on the importance of the *sensus fidelium*, brought to the fore by Newman, which was central to the mediaeval view, and which continues to be that of the Orthodox churches, has a place in Vatican 2. It is, however, in the second statement on authority from ARCIC that it becomes prominent. After stating that it is Christ himself, the Way, the Truth and the Life, who entrusts the Gospel to us and gives his Church a teaching authority which claims our obedience, the document says, 'The church as a whole, indwelt by the Spirit according to Christ's promise and looking to the testimony of the prophets, saints and martyrs of every generation, is witness, teacher and guardian of the truth.'[17] After asserting that general councils can make judgements to clarify the content of revelation, it goes on to say:

> The Church in all its members is involved in such a definition which clarifies and enriches their grasp of the truth. Their active reflection upon the definition in its turn clarifies its significance. Moreover, although it is not through reception by the people of God that a definition first acquires authority, the assent of the faithful is the ultimate indication that the Church's authoritative decision in a matter of faith has been truly preserved from error by the Holy Spirit. The Holy Spirit who maintains the Church in the truth will bring its members to receive the definition as true and to assimilate it if what has been declared genuinely expounds the revelation.[18]

This placing of the question of infallibility within the widest possible context, the Church as a whole, is extremely important from an ecumenical point of view. It may in the end allow the insights of the reformed churches to be accepted by the Roman Catholic Church as a contributing factor to the truth in its completeness. For the Roman Catholic Church is more and more willing to acknowledge a common baptism with other Christians. In the service in Canterbury Cathedral on 29 May 1982 there was a renewal of baptismal vows in which the Pope shared with Christians of other denominations. If the Koinonia of Christians is based on a common baptism then the partial truths affirmed in the traditions of the different denominations can be seen, and will more and more come to be seen, as part of the truth of the whole body.

The significance of a shared, mutually accepted baptism cannot be underestimated. As Clifford Longley wrote in *The Times*,

> The fundamental sacrament is baptism, again undergoing fundamental changes in emphasis. It was once

the key to the distinctive exclusivity of the Roman Catholic Church, as if Roman Catholic baptism was a special kind of baptism. It is now the key to Roman Catholic relations with other churches, whose members are now acknowledged without question as fellow Christians by virtue of baptism. It is a shift in perception of earthquake proportions, so fundamental that any prediction of its long-term significance would be foolish. Where once it excluded, it now includes. Christians of other churches have suddenly become regarded as honorary Catholics.[19]

This statement may not be a reliable guide to the theology of baptism, past or present, but it accurately records the dramatic shift in the way baptism has been viewed and administered at a parish level.

Perhaps it was because of this shift to an understanding of the Church and her authority which is all-inclusive that the Sacred Congregation for the Doctrine of the Faith, the special body of people in the Vatican whose responsibility it is to safeguard the faith, were not entirely happy about ARCIC's statement on authority. In *Observations*, their comment on the work of ARCIC, one of the points that they made concerned 'Reception'. They noted that Anglicans believe that if a papal judgement is not manifestly a legitimate interpretation of biblical faith they 'would think it is a duty to reserve the reception of the definition for study and discussion'.[20] Again they note ARCIC's view that 'reception by the faithful [is] a factor which must contribute, under the heading of an "ultimate" or "final" indication, to the recognition of the authority and value of the definition as a genuine expression of the faith.' They then comment that this view is not in accord with either the teaching of Vatican 1 or Vatican 2. In defence of ARCIC it can be said that the references to Vatican 2 are selective. They do not mention the *sensus fidelium* which characterizes the Church as a whole, not only the Pope and bishops. Do they have a too narrow understanding of the teaching authority of the Church?

Vatican 2 said, 'The task of authentically interpreting the word of God, whether written or handed on, has been entrusted exclusively to the living teaching office of the Church.'[21] This living teaching office cannot be identified exclusively with the Pope and bishops. It would imply a sharp division between the professionals who teach and the rest who are taught. Yet laypeople witness to Christ not just by what they do but by their Christian reflections. These reflections, which they contribute to the debates of the Church, help to shape the teaching of the Magisterium.

There is a genuine dilemma here, which ARCIC recognized. On the one hand, the authority of a revealed truth is not derived from or dependent on its recognition as such. On the other hand, if it is indeed a revealed *truth*, it would be very odd if it were not, in due course, recognized as such. In theory it is possible to imagine the Pope asserting the truth of some teaching for generations in the face of an unresponsive Church (he could be a new *Athanasius contra mundum*). In practice it is more likely that the Church's teaching will in the end reflect the views of the Church as a whole. Disapproval of usury, once universally taught to be contrary to Christ, was quietly dropped; the same could happen to the prohibition on artificial means of contraception, a prohibition which is now widely ignored in practice.

Reception is not a concept that concerns only Anglicans. Clifford Longley wrote in *The Times*, 'It would be extremely difficult to trace a single official statement of the Roman Catholic Church in England and Wales in the last decade that said anything at all about contraception. There is an embarrassed silence. Many priests, the majority of Roman Catholic laypeople, and even possibly most bishops in this country do not support their church's official teaching.' In the same article he pointed out that 'the catholic birthrate has fallen to the point where it is not significantly different from the rest of the population.' Also, when at a recent synod in Rome the Pope said that divorced Catholics in second marriages could not receive the sacraments unless they lived chastely as brother and sister, it was noted that 'Cardinal Hume, needless to say, has not passed the instruction on to his flock.' Here we see reception, or rather, non-reception, at work. No one wants to say that the truth of some doctrine or moral teaching depends upon its acceptance. Nevertheless, the experience and reflection of the Church as a whole play an integral part in expressing the truth of Christ. Inevitably and rightly the practical wisdom of laypeople makes a contribution to the formulation of teaching; and equally inevitably time itself provides a test.

'To live is to change.' The Church is a living body that provides teaching and guidance for its members in each generation. This teaching and guidance then takes its place as part of the tradition, to provide guidance to succeeding generations for subsequent formulations. To claim that this teaching and guidance is infallible is to claim that it has been kept from error. Newman was hostile to the Roman Catholic understanding of this in his Oxford Movement days; but it has been argued here that at the heart of infallibility is a profoundly religious notion that needs to be taken seriously by Christians of all persuasions. Nevertheless, there are two crucial and closely linked questions. One has to do with the place of the *sensus fidelium*. If, as has been suggested here, the responsibility for preserving and teaching Christian truth is not solely in the hands of an elite professional core but is in some measure shared by all Christian people; and if baptism, whoever performs it, is accepted as the defining mark of a Christian, then the way is open for regarding the whole Christian tradition, and not just the clerical Roman Catholic part, as contributing to the fullness of truth. The other question has to do with the place of reception. If reception is given a prominent place in the task of ascertaining the mind of Christ, then again the whole concept of infallibility becomes much wider and richer.

7 Indefectibility and Infallibility

One of the many remarkable features of the second ARCIC document on authority was its extreme reluctance to use the word infallibility. 'We agree,' it states, 'that this is a term applicable unconditionally only to God, and to use it of a human being, even in highly restricted circumstances, can produce many misunderstandings. That is why in stating our belief in the preservation of the Church from error we have avoided using the term' (ARCIC, A II, 32). The Commission preferred the word 'indefectibility'. 'The Church is confident that the Holy Spirit will effectually enable it to fulfil its mission so that it will neither lose its essential character nor fail to reach its goal' (ARCIC, A II, 23). A footnote adds, 'This is the meaning of *indefectibility*, a term which does not speak of the Church's lack of defects but confesses that, despite all its many weaknesses and failures, Christ is faithful to his promise that the gates of hell shall not prevail against it.' This note speaks of weaknesses and failures.

The first document on authority also mentioned the possibility of errors. When it stated that the bishops had a special responsibility for promoting truth and discerning error it said,

> But there is no guarantee that those who have an everyday responsibility will – any more than other members – invariably be free from errors of judgement, will never tolerate abuses, and will never distort the truth. Yet, in Christian hope, we are confident that such failures cannot destroy the Church's ability to proclaim the Gospel, and to show forth the Christian

> life; for we believe that Christ will not desert his Church and that the Holy Spirit will lead it into all truth. That is why the Church, in spite of its failures, can be described as indefectible (ARCIC, A I, 18).

It was not altogether a surprise that *Observations* was critical. In relation to the passage just quoted it said, 'One must note first of all that the term indefectibility, which ARCIC uses, is not equivalent to the term retained by the first Vatican council' (*Observations*, III, (3)). In other words, *Observations* wants to assert that the Church is both indefectible and infallible, the words referring to different ways in which Christ preserves his Church in the truth.

The word indefectible, though it sounds somewhat technical and formidable, goes the heart of the Christian faith, and what it is trying to convey would be believed by nearly all Christian people. It is a term of faith, rather than dogma; it points to the sermon rather than the text-book for its context. This, for example, is what Kung means by the word.

> The Church is distinguished from other human organizations – and this distinction is vital – only by the promise given to it as the community of believers in Christ; the promise that it will survive all errors and sins, that its truth will remain imperishable and indestructible through all storms, that the message of Jesus Christ will endure in it, that Jesus Christ will remain with it in spirit and thus keep it in the truth through all errors and confusion. . . . The Church may forsake her God; he will not forsake her. On her path through time she may go astray, may stumble and often even fall, she may fall among thieves and be left lying for dead. Yet, God will not abandon her, but will pour oil on her wounds, raise her up, and pay also what could not be foreseen for her healing. So the Church will continue on her way, living on the forgiveness, the healing and the strengthening of her Lord.[1]

This is an affirmation of faith that moves people, that leads them to have a firmer confidence in Christ; that enables them to commit themselves more joyfully to him. It is a statement that could be preached in any church of any denomination. What then is the difference between this and the concept of infallibility, if, as the *Observations* suggests, they are not identical? Three differences may be noticed; three differences of emphasis. First, indefectibility is concerned with the Christian life as a whole, and not just the formulation of its beliefs. Infallibility is concerned primarily with propositions. Secondly, indefectibility takes the long-term view. It allows for errors in the short term, and has confidence that in the end the Holy Spirit will lead the Church to correct them. Infallibility suggests that certain particular propositions are preserved from error both in the short term and the long term. Thirdly, indefectibility stresses the presence of Christ and the Holy Spirit with the Church *in and through* all the Church's wanderings and failures. Infallibility emphasizes the power of Christ and the Holy Spirit to preserve the Church *from* wanderings and failures, in matters of fundamental truth.

So *Observations* was probably right to suggest that indefectibility and infallibility are not equivalents. The former should be accepted by any Christian as an inescapable implication of his commitment to Christ. The latter is open to question. Nevertheless, some further progress in appreciating the notion can be made. In recent years Hans Kung has been the most outspoken critic of infallibility, but in stating his case Kung overstates it. He is hostile to the propositional element in the Christian faith. He stresses, rightly, that Christian faith is about faith in Christ himself. At its heart is a relationship and a commitment which goes beyond what can be conveyed in words. Nevertheless as was argued in chapter 2, propositions are inevitable and proper. Knowing someone and knowing certain facts about them (faith in and faith that) are inseparably intertwined. I trust my friend because I believe him to be trustworthy. I can make the assertion 'He is trustworthy' because when asked for reasons to back up my belief I can adduce facts that I have observed about him. We put our trust in God, the faithful one, and this assertion is enlarged in a set of propositions, some doctrinal and some factual, that we call the creed. Although propositions should be seen in the context of our relationship to God, that relationship involves some doctrinal formulation. The confession of Peter, 'You are the Christ' (paradigmatic for discipleship) is itself a proposition. Christianity is committed to the truth of certain propositions.

In pointing out the errors of various allegedly ecumenical church councils, Kung offers nothing between error in the short term and a conviction that the Holy Spirit will see the Church through in the very long run, that is, will preserve it from hell. It is true that, as Kung points out, in the first centuries of the Church's history one council corrected or amended the work of another, but what are we to say of that period as a whole? What are we to say of that great work of Christian formulation, the doctrines of God as Holy Trinity and the Incarnation, that went on for the first seven centuries of the Church's life? Was it mistaken or was it not? It is easy to pick out certain councils which were set up as ecumenical but which were not recognized as such by the Church as a whole. It is easy to point to views, accepted at one council, which were rejected or altered at a later one. But still the central question remains. Was the broad sweep of the doctrinal development in error? Were the central formulations made at that time, over centuries of anguish and struggle, true or false? Were they made under the guidance of the Holy Spirit, or were they simply one line of development that the Church happened to take, when it could, without losing its identity, have taken another? If a small enough time scale is taken it is easy enough to show up flaws and apparent contradictions, but there is no doubt that over a period the Church as a body committed itself to the truth of certain definite propositions.

Christians cannot eliminate the propositional element from their faith, and there is no good reason why they should want to do so. But there are important qualifications. The articles of the creed and decisions of the councils, however dry and formal they may sometimes appear, are in the end doxological: they open out into praise and glorifying of God. They are primarily intended to be the end point of a discussion, rather than the basis for future statements. The flavour is well caught by the affirmation in the Nicene Creed that Christ is 'God of God, Light of Light, Very God of Very God'. In this sentence an article of faith merges into an act of praise; this is, in principle, the character of all the major Christian assertions.[2]

God is beyond human language. We can speak about him in analogy and we do so, when it is not to praise, only to block off false views. St Hilary of Poitiers put it marvellously: 'The errors of heretics and blasphemers force us to deal with unlawful matters, to scale perilous heights, to speak unutterable words, to trespass on forbidden ground. Faith ought in silence to fulfil the commandments, worshipping the Father, reverencing with him the Son, abounding in the Holy Spirit . . . the error of others compels us to err in daring to embody in human terms truths which ought to be hidden in the silent veneration of the heart.'[3]

Indefectibility says that despite errors the Holy Spirit preserves the Church in the truth. Infallibility, on the other hand, suggests that certain specific propositions have been preserved from error. Karl Rahner began his essay on the subject with the words, 'What we mean is the dogma of infallibility in its traditional sense, in which it actually refers to the truth of the *individual* defined proposition as such, and so not *merely* in the sense in which, for instance, H. Kung and W. Kaspar seem to interpret it.'[4]

There are different kinds of difficulty raised by the view that particular propositions are infallible. Some of these are inevitable. Propositions have to be transplanted, and the difficulties of finding an exact equivalent in another language are notorious. Unless, however, infallibility entails the verbal inerrancy of the original language, as it does in Islam with its written commitment to the Arabic of the Koran, those equivalents have to be searched for; not least because Christians are commanded to preach the Gospel to the ends of the earth. Perhaps in most cases the difficulty is not too great. But some cultures differ radically from our own. Rodney Needham found that the Penan people of Borneo were so sure of the existence of a supreme spiritual being that they had no way in which their language could compose such a statement as 'I believe in God'. He found the same situation among the Meru of Kenya and commented, 'There might be no point in providing lexically for the assertion "I believe in God" when God's existence and presence are so taken for granted that no other possibility is either given in Meru collective ideation or occasioned in individual thought.'[5]

Talk of distant places like Borneo and Kenya should remind us of the real differences that exist even in European culture between one age and another, and between one country and another. The result is that the truth of a proposition cannot be conveyed simply by literal translation from one language to another. Nor can it be done simply by discovering, through the work of historians, exactly what the words meant to the people who first formulated the belief. The matter goes deeper than that. There is a fundamental truth in the original proposition which has to be grasped anew in our terms. We say in the creed 'I believe in God, the father almighty, maker of heaven and earth.' When people said that in the fourteenth or the eighth centuries, or when they had Genesis read to them, the pictures going through their minds were different from the ones that go through ours. We think of an exploding universe in which the Earth is a tiny dot, and of the slow emergence of life through a long process of evolution. But we can still believe and affirm in the creed that the universe, however it came into being, whether through an explosion at the beginning of time or through the continuous creation of matter, is fundamentally dependent, moment by moment, for its existence, on God.

We can distinguish three basic attitudes to propositions. We can seek the literal truth or the subjective mythological truth or the essential truth. The difference can be seen in relation to another statement in the creed: 'I believe in the resurrection of the body.' The literalist believes that at the end of time the physical constituents of our body will be reassembled and transformed. The subjective mythological approach suggests that this was the way human beings felt about the universe when the creed was formulated and that we now feel differently. The essential truth of the notion has to do with God's recreation of our essential self after death so that there is both continuity and discontinuity with the person we are now.

The literalistic view and the subjective mythological attitude are mirror images of each other. The subjective mythological approach takes the literal meaning, rejects it as literally true but accepts it as the way people interpreted the universe at the time when the belief was first formulated, the emphasis being on the way man saw life rather than on any objective truth about the universe revealed through the myth. The essentialist position is that there is a fundamental truth revealed, even though some of the ways in which we conceptualize it may be different from the way it was conceptualized when the belief was first formulated. The essentialist position allows for the truth in past formulations to be retained and at the same time restated if necessary.

In the history of the Church there are many examples of restatement or reinterpretation that have failed to retain the truth expressed in the original formulation. There are also many examples of successful restatement. In the 1960s, as a result of the influence of the verification principle in linguistic philosophy, some Christians tried to restate their understanding of the centrality of Christ in different terms. Professor Braithwaite, for example, expressed it in terms of a personal commitment evoked and nourished by the story of Jesus, which gave a particular perspective on the world. Professor Van Buren from American went through the Nicene Creed article by article, restating the articles in terms of perspective and personal commitment.

These bold attempts were probably judged by most Christians to have failed, in that they did not conserve the essence of what the original meant. On the other hand, many changes have taken place in our understanding of Christ, such as an awareness of his human limitations and lack of knowledge, and the fact that he was schooled and conditioned by the culture of his time. These changes have deepened our appreciation of what it involves for God to become truly man. It is possible to do full justice to the humanity of Christ, a humanity that shares to the full the limitations and weaknesses of us all, and at the same time affirm that he is truly the eternal Son of God made man. The German theologian W. Pannenberg does just this. He begins from the New Testament picture of Jesus as a man called by God to proclaim the Kingdom of God, and uses all the critical tools of modern biblical scholarship; and he finds the two-natures language of the Council of Chalcedon unhelpful. Nevertheless, as the title of his book, *Jesus God and Man*, indicates, he works through to a fully orthodox conclusion.

This approach, which works on the assumption that it is possible to restate the faith in a way that is true to the past, underlies the work of ARCIC. It has produced some remarkable results; for example, on the nature of the Eucharist. But what about the Marian dogmas that at present divide Anglicans and Roman Catholics? These dogmas would generally be classed among those termed irreformable. ARCIC II says, 'The term "irreformable" means that the truth expressed in the definition can no longer be questioned. "Irreformable" does not mean that the definition is the Church's last word on the matter and that the definition cannot be restated in other terms.' Karl Rahner has pointed out, rightly, that the technical language of theology is the language of analogy. This means that it is possible both to affirm and to deny the same proposition provided the negation is not simply intended as a formal denial of the affirmation. The example he gives is 'There is such a thing as original sin' and 'There is no such thing as original sin'. Both these assertions could be true; for the second need not be a denial of the first but the positive assertion of another aspect of the truth.[6]

Given a desire to extract the kernel of truth from its

cultural and linguistic husk and an awareness that all theological language is analogous, how far is it possible to go in reaching agreement on the Marian dogmas? A note in ARCIC II states about Mary: 'The affirmation that her glory in heaven involves full participation in the fruits of salvation expresses and reinforces our faith that the life of the world to come has already broken into the life of our world.' With this statement few Christians would disagree. But the doctrine of the Assumption of the Blessed Virgin Mary has traditionally asserted that after her death she was assumed body and soul into heaven, that her body was not found. Is the Church committed to the alleged fact that her body no longer remained on this earth? Austin Farrer, a man sympathetic to infallibility, stated that alleged facts must be open to the historian. They cannot be created by any ecclesiastical authority, 'for history, including Catholic history, is corrigible; and what is corrigible cannot be called infallible.' So 'I shall need to be assured that the utterances which dogmatized the immaculate conception and the corporeal assumption need not be held incorrigible. It is this sort of thing that frightens me so much; in those two decrees we have the alarming appearance of an infallible fact-factory going full blast.'[7] That Mary fully participates in the fruits of salvation and that she lives in glory in heaven, can legitimately be pronounced by ecclesiastical authority and can be judged to be consonant with holy scripture, even if not fully developed in it. But whether Mary was buried like other human beings or whether she was assumed body and soul into heaven, is a matter for historians.

Roman Catholic theologians today make it possible for many outside their communion to have a sympathetic understanding of the doctrine of the Assumption of the Blessed Virgin Mary. According to Edward Yarnold it means that 'all that is truly of value in human existence continues after death, when it is transformed in heaven.' Bishop Butler says that 'Our Lady enjoys in virtue of her close union with her Son, that fullness of bliss which we all hope to enjoy after the final resurrection.' Father Richards wrote, 'It means that *now* Mary *as a complete person* is in heaven.' He regards the doctrine as a statement in personal terms of the doctrine of Justification: 'Mary enjoys the destiny of every Christian and received the grace of Justification/Sanctification from the beginning of her life, to fit her for being Mother of God. Otherwise human effort would have opened the way to salvation – which must be entirely from God.'

These statements imply that if the body of Mary was unearthed by excavators the essential truth of the belief would not be touched. But does the original declaration allow this liberty? Vatican 2 said that, 'The Immaculate Virgin was taken up body and soul into heavenly glory'. This statement referred to the Papal Bull *Munificentissimus* of 1 November 1950, in which the doctrine was officially defined. This asserted that after Mary had finished the course of her earthly life 'fuisse corpore et anima ad caelstem gloriam assumptam'. Is this language compatible with believing that Mary's bones might still be on earth? There is a parallel with the resurrection of Christ, where there are two aspects to the question. There is a historical question, whether or not the tomb of Jesus was empty; and there is a faith question, whether Jesus was raised from the dead. It is possible to believe the latter without believing the former, though for most of Christian history the two have been regarded as mutually interdependent. There is also a factual question about belief in Mary's corporeal assumption. It is part of the mercy and mystery of the incarnation that the eternal Son of God became part of the flow of history and subjected himself to what is contingent, even to the extent of investigation by historians. The same applies to Mary.

It is obvious from what has been written in this and the previous chapter that the concept of infallibility held by the Church and the view of it as pictured in the popular mind are utterly different. The popular caricature of infallibility sees it as belonging to the Pope alone, and fears he might suddenly be inspired to promulgate new doctrines with no basis in the Bible. The proper understanding of infallibility, however, is that it belongs to the Church as a whole, not to the Pope in isolation; and its function is not to discover new doctrines but to ensure that the truth revealed once and for all in Christ is faithfully interpreted and transmitted. Nevertheless, there is a legitimate worry behind the popular caricature, which is the concern of theologians of all communions. Both the doctrine of the Immaculate Conception and the doctrine of the Assumption were pronounced by the Pope alone, without benefit of the council of bishops. However strongly grounded in tradition such beliefs might be, however strong the popular pressure for their promulgation, Anglicans and Orthodox, together with very many Roman Catholics, believe that such independence is a denial of the properly collegial and collaborative nature of the papacy.

The Church is a living, developing body. In each generation it has been forced to make decisions about what is and what is not consonant with its identity as the catholic church. Roman Catholics believe that on fundamental matters the Holy Spirit has kept the Church from error in these decisions. This and the previous chapters have noted the fundamentally religious, rather than polemical, motive which leads people to believe in infallibility: it has observed how the concept of a *sensus fidelium* is enlarging the idea of the Magisterium of the Church so that 'the Truth' is seen to belong to the body as a whole and is not the exclusive preserve of the episcopacy: it has distinguished between indefectibility and infallibility. Although Anglicans, like Newman in his early days, and people like Austin Farrer, have wanted to affirm the idea of indefectibility and have remained suspicious of the other, we have found it possible to go some way to a sympathetic grasp of the notion of infallibility as well.

There is an essential propositional element in the Christian faith. Furthermore, it is possible to restate the formulations of the past in a new way which both preserves the truth they are trying to express and also balances that truth by another if this is necessary. No authority can make a fact out of what is not a fact, and all alleged facts must be open to investigation by ordinary historical methods. Nevertheless the Church does have authority to pronounce on what is and what is not a legitimate development of what lies latent in the New Testament. In deciding what is and what is not consistent with the faith, as it has developed over the centuries, it will, over a period of time, be kept from error. The difficult question is: over what period of time? The Marian dogmas, which many Christians find difficult, were defined during a period of about a century and a half of intense Marian devotion, some of it deliberately encouraged for political purposes. It took several centuries for the full truth of the Trinity and Incarnation to emerge in the early Church. There is more yet to be said on the Marian dogmas, both on their definition and their place within the hierarchy of Christian truths. Christians who are not Roman Catholics would want to emphasize that these doctrines were not pronounced by a truly ecumenical council, and that the corporate mind of the Church as a whole has yet to express itself on their validity.

8 The Anglican Heritage

Stephen Sykes has written, 'If one compares the present situation with the pre-Oxford Movement Church of England, it is patent that within the last 150 years there has taken place the most profound process of deconfessionalization to fall upon any European denomination.'[1] He points to the demotion of the Prayer Book and articles and the new declaration and oath of assent 'hospitable of a wider variety of opinion than any previous oath'. The context in which the ARCIC documents are discussed has to be taken into account. 'All churches are, by definition, confessing bodies; and Anglicanism seems to be in a strange twilight zone between a confessing past and a future of some unspecific kind.' These judgements seem to me correct, and it is worth looking, however briefly, at the reasons for this deconfessionalization.

We should note the continuing influence of the Evangelical revival at the end of the eighteenth century and of successive Evangelical renewals. The prime passion of Evangelicals has been that people should become truly converted and commit their lives to Christ the risen, living Lord who has redeemed them personally from sin. For this reason Evangelicals within the Church of England have often felt more at home with Evangelicals whatever their denomination, than in the average gathering of Anglicans. At university level, for example, the influence of the Inter-Varsity Fellowship has been extensive over many generations. In this Fellowship, with its branches in all the various universities, Anglican Evangelicals, have played a prominent role. Certainly in the early years after becoming a member of one of these groups a person is likely to feel that he is an Evangelical first and an Anglican second, and to act on this assumption. It is true that Evangelicals have defended the thirty-nine articles and argued for their retention because, so they believe, it is a way of ensuring that the Church of England remains Protestant. But this has been a defensive measure. They have no enthusiasm for the articles. They are too dry, too formal, too dated for most Evangelicals, particularly those who have been caught up in the Charismatic movement.

What is true of Evangelical Anglicans is no less true of Anglicans of a Catholic persuasion. Newman defended a Catholic interpretation of the thirty-nine articles and his successors have always argued that the Church of England is part of the one Holy, Catholic and Apostolic Church; that part of the Catholic Church which is in this land, in unbroken line with the Church in England before the Reformation. But again, Catholic-minded Anglicans have not fully supported the thirty-nine articles or the Prayer Book. It is true that some Anglican Catholics have in recent years been among the staunchest defenders of the Prayer Book, but it has not been the Prayer Book unadulterated. Rather, the Prayer Book has been used selectively, within the context of Catholic ritual, and as often as not with at least some of the illegal 1928 book, which was an attempt to reform the 1662 book to admit Catholic features. Within Catholic Anglicanism some have looked unashamedly to Rome and have either celebrated or attended the Roman Mass. Others, less extreme, have still regarded themselves as members of the Catholic Church first and Anglicans second. So this sizeable body of people, over the last hundred years the dominant group within the Church of England, have not had their heart in it. Their heart has been within the whole Catholic tradition; and they have felt happy to remain within the Church of England only in so far as they have been able to square its traditions with what has been regarded as the mainstream of Catholic Christianity.

There is another group which should not be forgotten. They are sometimes dismissed with labels like liberal or modernist or radical, but within this group, which overlaps to some extent with the other two, there has been the dominant motive of intellectual integrity. They have grappled with the fundamental questions of human existence and the major doctrines of the faith. Men like F.D. Maurice, William Temple and the late Ian Ramsey, Bishop of Durham, may fairly be said to belong to this tradition. While some of them have been stalwart defenders of the Church of England, like William Temple, and they have on the whole felt happy in it, they have not been fully devoted to it. Their interest has been in fundamental, rather than ecclesiastical matters, and the Church of England has provided the liberty in which these can be thought about and talked about with integrity.

These features of Anglicanism raise questions about its so-called comprehensiveness and liberality; questions not about the existence of these qualities but about their value and what it is that they are really rooted in. Is Anglican comprehensiveness anything more than a pragmatic device for keeping very different groups within the one fold, groups whose true identity is found and formed elsewhere? It certainly remains true that Anglicanism is groping its way forward to 'a future of some unspecified kind'.

What worries Professor Sykes is that in reaching out to a joint future with Rome the Church of England may find its own formularies in danger of being overriden and superseded: 'Does not the whole of the ARCIC movement represent a reconfessionalization of Anglicanism? Anglican ordinands, who scarcely give a passing thought to the Thirty Nine Articles in their training for the ministry, are apparently invited by ARCIC to attend to the precise meaning of passages from the decrees of Vatican 1 and 2.' Furthermore, although the ARCIC documents give a place to Anglican formularies and traditions, if a conflict emerged in some future united church the Pope could instruct a diocesan bishop and expect to be obeyed. What then would happen to the Anglican inheritance? 'The traditions (and freedom) which Anglicans value are not to be surrendered. The major problem is for Rome to decide whether such freedom, against the exercise of which it has so strenuously campaigned in recent episodes, is now to be regarded as inherent in the very catholicity of the Church.'

But what is this tradition and what are these freedoms? As already mentioned, the Anglican tradition is in a state of flux. Over the last 150 years it has become deconfessionalized. All traditions within the Church of England are groping their way to a new future. We have to ask whether the much vaunted comprehensiveness and liberality of the Church of England has been anything more than a method of keeping groups with strongly differing views from tearing the Church apart. This was the nature of the Elizabethan settlement. It succeeded then and it has succeeded down the years. But it is not satisfactory as a final resting place. The problem is not simply that outside critics judge the Church of England to be too indefinite. It is that its most committed members, of all traditions, would like to shape the Church in accord with their own vision. Their vision may vary less now than in the past but all would agree in wanting something better than the present: a clearer outline of belief and teaching, a deeper unity.

By freedom Sykes means not only the willingness of different traditions to inhabit the same house but also freedom of intellectual inquiry. He is worried about the disciplining of Roman Catholic theologians. He believes that critics must be allowed if there is to be a genuine consensus in the Church, as opposed to authority believing it has the consent of everyone. But critics are 'marginalized by being removed from positions of influence, especially in the Universities'. Yet it can hardly be said that Kung and Schillebeeckx, who have been disciplined, have lost influence. Kung has been deprived of his title as an official theologian of the Roman Catholic Church but he retains his university chair, he lectures and his books are read all over the world. The word 'freedom' is a large but vague word. It needs to be qualified. Freedom to do or teach what? To ask the question is to see that freedom to teach or do some things is incompatible with holding an official position in the Church. To take an extreme example, it would be odd if the Archbishop of Canterbury suddenly announced that the Buddha was the most important religious figure the world has known. Any group that is going to retain its identity needs certain boundaries. If it teaches everything it teaches nothing. The New Testament makes it quite clear that certain beliefs and certain kinds of behaviour are incompatible with membership of the Christian Church. If a recognized Christian teacher begins to teach what is incompatible with the faith, his recognition may be withdrawn. In that way the Church makes it clear what it believes and what it stands for.

In August 1982 the World Alliance of Reformed Churches in Ottawa condemned Apartheid as a heresy and formally suspended the two major white branches of the Dutch Reformed Church in South Africa. Who would doubt that the Church must make it clear where it stands on this issue? But this is not the only case needing censure. This seems a very un-Anglican thing to write, because we are suspicious of any infringement of personal liberty and we fear witch-hunts. The heresy hunts in all denominations have indeed been an appalling blot on the Church.

Liberty of conscience is indeed sacred. But theologians whose work is censured, or whose title is withdrawn, are still at liberty to speak and write. What they are not at liberty to do, is to do this in the name of the Church. A theologian may disagree with a judgement in a particular case. He may claim that what he teaches is compatible with the faith, that it is not a jettisoning of some belief but a legitimate reinterpretation of it. Although he may argue in this way he cannot deny the right of the Church to make it clear what is and what is not Christian teaching. For the vocation of a theologian is to serve the Church. He is not a rootless intellectual but a servant of the truth that he has received. Pope John Paul II issued an Apostolic Constitution on Ecclesiastical Universities and Faculties (Sapientia Christiana, 15 April 1979) which emphasized the adherence of faculties of theology 'to the full doctrine of Christ, whose authentic guardian and interpreter has always been through the Magisterium of the Church'. Anglican theologians, like Roman Catholic ones, are members of the Church first and theologians second. Their vocation, a very high one, is still one vocation among many, all of which seek in different ways to bring about the fullness of Christ.

We blanch at the possibility of Anglican theologians, or their writings, being censured because we confuse liberty of speech (which they would continue to have) with liberty to teach anything under the sun in the name of the Church; but also because the Church has so often been disastrously wrong in what it has censured. Sometimes the fact that a person has been censured is almost a sign that he must be right, the fact that a book has been banned almost an advertisement that it contains some important truth that must be read at all costs. Yet the fact that the Church's judgement in the past has often been faulty does not take away its right to make such judgements. It makes us suspicious of its judgements but we admit its right to make them, just as an individual has the right to say that certain actions are incompatible with his own deepest understanding of himself.

Within Anglicanism the Gospel has been construed with the help of certain Patristic writings and a number of sixteenth- and seventeenth-century liturgies and documents. Sykes is concerned that in the ARCIC report this tradition does not have equal weight with the Roman Catholic one. 'Whatever Roman Catholic texts are interpreted, they are interpreted in the most Anglican sense conceivable. On the other hand, many Anglicans will be very astonished to discover that *these* texts and documents have become so formative in the consideration of subjects like Authority and Ministry.' He fears that there might be a strong presumption in favour of Roman confessional documentation. In this case, 'then two Anglican theological traditions deriving respectively from the reformation and from the enlightenment, and both with their roots in Scripture, are in some doubt.'

Behind this criticism there seems to lie an assumption

that theological traditions are static, whereas both the Anglican and Roman traditions are in a state of rapid development. Anglicanism, as Sykes recognizes from his talk of deconfessionalization, has changed dramatically over the last 150 years as a result of the fresh faith and vision of Catholics, Evangelicals and agonizers over the truth. It is moving into a new future. So, no less, is Roman Catholicism, and the shifts ever since Vatican 2 have been remarkable. The most significant way in which both have undergone change, in such a way as to bring them closer to one another, is through the common acceptance of the historico-critical method. As ARCIC put it, 'For a considerable period theologians of our two traditions, without compromising their respective allegiances, have worked on common problems with the same methods. In the process they have come to see old problems in new horizons and have experienced a theological convergence which has often taken them by surprise.' (ARCIC, AI, 25.) 'The enlightenment' mentioned by Sykes does not consist of a few documents; it is an attitude to the quest for truth. It is reflected in the critical study of the Bible and other ancient documents; and this in turn is reflected in the ARCIC documents. The same is true, if in a less marked way, of the Reformation. The ARCIC statement on the Eucharist said, 'Christ's redeeming death and resurrection took place once and for all in history. Christ's death on the cross, the culmination of his whole life of obedience, was the one, perfect and sufficient sacrifice for the sins of the world. There can be no repetition of or addition to what was then accomplished once and for all by Christ.' This is not only one of the trumpet calls of the reformers; it is the very phrasing of the 1662 Eucharistic Prayer.

Some years ago K.J. Woollcombe (later Bishop Woollcombe) wrote that Anglican Catholics in America had tended to accept the Puseyite notion of infallibility and that they were mistaken to do so. He himself argued against that view and called Dean Church as a witness to the attitude which, he believed, should have prevailed within Anglicanism. Dean Church is worth quoting, 'as an example of that devout loyalty to the Anglican tradition which Dean Church, alone of the Oxford men, maintained in its entirety.'[2]

> Without infallibility, it is said, men will turn freethinkers and heretics; but don't they *with* it? . . . Meanwhile truth does stay in the world . . . yet we seem to receive that message as we receive the witness of moral truth; and it would not be contrary to the analogy of things here if we had often got to it at last through mistakes. But when it is reached, there it is, strong in its own power; and it is difficult to think that if it is not strong enough in itself to stand, it can be protected by a claim of infallibility.[3]

This is a fine passage, and it is indeed true that Catholic truth is strong enough to stand in its own power. But it is not the purpose of infallibility to stop people turning into freethinkers and heretics. Infallibility is the expression of a religious faith that God will guide his Church, that he will keep it in the truth. People may reject it, heretics may break away from it; but it is God's purpose that there should remain in the world a recognizable body of truth that can lay claim to be the legitimate interpretation and development of the faith once delivered to the saints.

In the end someone who has been sympathetic to the argument so far is presented with a dilemma that does not admit of easy rational solution. He can affirm boldly that the Church is infallible, that she is kept from error on fundamental matters of faith and morals, and then proceed to define, and hence qualify, what it means to call the Church infallible. These qualifications are more stringent than are generally recognized. Bishop Butler, discussing the infallibility of the Pope, poses the question of what would happen if the Pope was wicked or insane. 'It can be held that, by the sin of heresy or schism, a duly elected Pope would, in fact, cease to be Pope; and that, if such circumstances arose, "the Church represented through an ecumenical council by human convocation" could declare that "the first see" was void and take steps for its replenishment.' Furthermore, 'As regards a Pope's possible insanity, it should be remarked that only the "human acts" of a Pope can claim validity. An insane act is not a human act.'[4] The weakness of this approach to infallibility is that, as Anthony Flew said about a bold brash assertion like 'God is love', it can die the death of a thousand qualifications. Closely connected with this is the need for a continuous reassessment and perhaps reinterpretation of the authoritative statements of the past. Some think this smacks of dishonesty. Such apologia, says Sykes, 'seems to put a premium on theologians of extreme legalistic subtlety capable of wresting modern-sounding meanings from documents of a past age; or alternatively those able to deploy fashionable hermeneutical gambits at once to justify and to relativize decisions of the past.'

On the other hand, we can boldly affirm that the Church in the past has made mistakes, that within any church there are bound to be different views, even about fundamentals; and that this is all part of the liberty of life in Christ. The question which has to be asked about this approach is whether anyone from outside the faith altogether has been attracted by this vision of Christianity? Anglicanism has its converts. Some are people who have been Roman Catholics, who know what the faith is in its essentials, and who want a slightly freer atmosphere in which to practise it either for intellectual reasons or because of the circumstances of their private lives. But those who come into the Church from the cold are usually converted either by Evangelicals or they are drawn by the vision of a Catholic Christianity (for example, T.S. Eliot). Anglicanism, as a vague all-embracing atmosphere, is a comfortable home to live in, and as an acquired taste for the sophisticated it appears a noble way, but it lacks the definiteness which is a mark of the faith in the New Testament.

This is not a justification of simple answers to complex questions nor is it a capitulation to the new authoritarianism: but the Church of England is on the move. It is recovering its sense of confidence and authority and is reaching out to a different future. The most significant cause of this is the sundering of some of the main links with Parliament. The Church now has the power to order its own worship and to legislate for its own life. Some people dislike what is happening. One well-known bishop boasted, after the Church had spent years revising its canon law, that he had never read the canons. For the preparation of this book I tried to obtain a copy of these canons in the library of an Anglican college: to no avail. There were canons from past centuries, but not the present revision. All this has a healthy side: the suspicion of legalism, the awareness that at its best the Church makes decisions on the basis of 'It seemed good to the Holy Spirit and to us.' Legalism has to be watched, and it is better if the Church spends time on the great issues that confront it rather than on re-ordering its internal life.

Nevertheless, in a time of flux it is not ignoble to get one's own house tidied up; it is not ignoble for a church that believes in the revelation of God in Christ to try to order its affairs with what it conceives to be the mind of Christ. The Church is on the way to a different future, and there is probably a greater degree of unity within it than for many years. This is not because of any specifically Christian spirit, for there is still much party sniping. The influence of the Liturgical Movement over a period of 100 years and of biblical scholarship has brought about a common mind on issues that divided the church fifty years ago. The reception of the Alternative Service Book compared with the 1928 book is the obvious example. Neverthe less it would be fatal at this time of growing confidence and authority for the Church of England to order its affairs as though it intended to remain a separated body. Its future lies within the Catholic Church as a whole.

The affirmation that the Church is infallible appeals to those who like matters definite. The affirmation that the nature of the Church is comprehensive appeals to those who feel that by this they are included rather than pushed outside because of their difficulties. These feelings are at a psychological level. At the theological level infallibility is rooted in the conviction that God has revealed himself and will continue to keep his Church in the truth. The vision of the Church as a body which is inclusive rather than exclusive is rooted in the love and respect with which Christ treats us. There is no denying that there will be some tension between these two convictions within the Church until God is seen face to face; but the judgement of this book is that the way forward indicated by ARCIC is not out of character for Anglicanism as it seeks a new future that is visibly within the wider fellowship of the Catholic Church.

There are difficulties, but none that cannot be overcome if the will is there. Many of these difficulties are about attitudes to the past. Two attitudes to the past have been contrasted, that which is willing to admit mistakes and that which seeks to reinterpret the past. Yet, when two people who have been estranged come together again with a new harmony, there is a sense in which the past drops away. They are not always harping on previous differences. We cannot escape entirely from our past nor should we want to, but we can move from the past treated as polemic to the past as a seed bed of a future unity. We are in continuous dialogue with our past; it is always in the process of being reassessed and re-interpreted.

The Roman Catholic Church has greater difficulties about its past in relation to Anglicanism than Anglicans have in relation to Roman Catholics. Roman Catholics have more normative documents and they are more closely tied to these than Anglicans are to their formularies. The problem is well brought out by a correspondent who drew my attention to some words uttered by Pope Paul VI on 20 June 1977 on the relationship between theologians and the Magisterium: 'Nor must it be forgotten that it is the whole of the documents of the Magisterium that are normative for doctrine. Even if their teaching can be completed or presented with new tones, it cannot be neglected, far less contradicted.' The correspondent went on to say: 'These very clear and emphatic Papal words should alert everyone to place no reliance at all on, say, the words of Bishop Alan Clark of East Anglia about Pope Leo XIII's *Apostolicae Curae* of September 1896; even though *Apostolicae Curae*, like *Mystici Corporis Christi*, is of course very much "a document of the Magisterium", Bishop Alan Clark publicly suggested that this document "could be left in a pigeon-hole to gather dust".'

Given the will, there are ways of proceeding with Anglicans that can avoid either simply restating *Apostolicae Curae* on the one hand or putting it in a pigeon-hole to gather dust on the other: and to this task the new Anglican/Roman Catholic commission will address itself.

It is not beyond the wit of Christians, Anglican or Roman Catholic, if their heart is in it, to see their respective pasts in a fresh light, and through the illumination cast thereby to affirm a common future. The emphasis must be on the heart and will to do this: for it is the authority of divine love that we both affirm, who in Christ has reached out and united us to himself, and to one another, within the life of the Blessed Trinity, to whom be praise now and always.

Postscript: Newman, Rome and the task today

The point of reference for much of this book has been Newman's *Lectures on the Prophetical Office of the Church viewed relatively to Romanism and Popular Protestantism*, in which he argued for the validity of an Anglican *via media* against the errors of both Protestantism and Roman Catholicism. Yet Newman did not remain an Anglican. He became a member of the church he had once so forthrightly denounced; he lost confidence in the catholicity of the church he had so stalwartly defended. If Newman, a man of such outstanding intellect and holiness, went that way, there inevitably arises the question whether we should not follow him.

In his *Apologia Pro Vita Sua* Newman set out his mental history from 1833 to 1945 and explained the reasons which led him to break with the Church of England. First, during his study of Church history he discovered that the party which at the time looked extreme turned out in the light of later Christian judgement to have been right. Both on the Arian question (when the divinity of Christ was debated) and in the Monophysite controversy (when the issue was the unity of the divine and human in Christ) it appeared that the compromise party, as well as the obviously heretical one, was wrong. With a jolt Newman saw a parallel to his own time. The Roman Catholic Church was extremist, the Anglican Church was trying to work out a compromise between it and Protestantism. Would the Anglican Church also turn out to be in error?

A distinction must be made between the psychological effect of this parallel on Newman and its validity for others.

It did indeed have an enormous effect on him, but in general there can be no conclusive argument from history along such lines. No situation in history is exactly like another and it is easier to draw false lessons from the past than it is to draw true ones. In particular the doctrinal discussions of the fourth and fifth centuries were a very different kind of dispute from the ones about authority in the nineteenth century. In the former, extremes were of the essence, for it was the paradox of the incarnation of God in man that was involved. The Church asserts that Jesus is both fully God and fully man. There is, however, no necessary extremism on the question of authority. Bodies with very definite, extreme views, which they promulgate with a conviction of total assurance, are not always right, to say the least.

Secondly, Newman found that Tract 90, in which he had argued for a catholic interpretation of the thirty-nine articles of the Book of Common Prayer, was bitterly attacked. In particular it was the bishops, who on Newman's theory were the guardians of the apostolicity of the Church of England, who were hostile to him. It made Newman feel that his church did not after all teach Catholic truth. Since Newman's time, however, the scene has changed so much. Within the Church of England the position for which Newman argued, the Catholic interpretation of the thirty-nine articles, soon became not only acceptable but dominant. The prevailing ethos of the Church of England over the last 100 years has been a liberal Catholicism.

Thirdly, Newman was distressed by the plan to appoint a bishop in Jerusalem in conjunction with the Lutherans. It was a dagger at the heart of his belief that the Church of England was part of the Catholic Church, not a Protestant sect. Although this incident was important for Newman it can hardly be taken as revealing the mind of the Church for all time.

The most important reason, however, why what seemed necessary to Newman may no longer strike us in the same light is that so much has happened since then. There have been dramatic changes in the last 150 years both within

Anglicanism and Roman Catholicism, and the relationship between the two churches has been transformed. Biblical scholarship, the liturgical movement, the acceptance of the historico-critical method and the sharp awareness of a crucial common task have ensured that both churches look at one another, and the old controversies, in a new way. Both churches have developed. The Oxford Movement transformed the Church of England. The Roman Catholic Church underwent a radical change as a result of Vatican 2, a change which on a number of crucial issues reflected the influence of Newman himself.

After resigning from the University Church of St Mary's in Oxford Newman went to Littlemore, where he lived in lay communion with the Church of England. There he thought through his position and tried to ensure that if he joined the Roman Catholic Church this would be a reasoned and not just an emotional decision. The result of this period of reflection was his essay on *The Idea of Development*.

> The essay was an exploration, but he came to feel that the idea of development was essential to the Church and it enabled him to see how, and sometimes why, ideas had grown up about the mother of Jesus, for instance, or the Eucharist, or the papal office, which were not corruptions but the result of collective pondering on what happened in Jesus the Christ. And because it was necessary to draw the line between reality and superstition, the need for such judgement had gradually defined the apostolic office of the bishops, with the Pope at their head – a collective responsibility, whether exercised in Council or individually. The Church was not a changeless idea; it was a living community. Christ was one and the same, but the understanding of him must grow as the collective mind of the human race grows in the search for truth; the guidance of the Spirit was promised to, and mediated through the united body. And St Peter's successor was the divinely appointed centre of unity.[1]

Newman's idea of development, summarized thus by Meriol Trevor, has transformed the relationships of the two churches. First, it helped them both to think developmentally. The old tendency to think of Christian truth as fixed and frozen has been melted. This has enabled many Anglicans to be more sympathetic to the whole developing Catholic tradition; and it has enabled many Roman Catholics to view their own doctrines in a new light. Secondly, it is quite obvious that both churches have changed and developed greatly in the last 150 years; and this change, together with the acceptance of the idea that development is a continuing feature of the life of the Church, not something that ended with the promulgation of the Marian dogmas has made both churches more sensitive to the possibility of real change.

One key development has concerned the Anglican attitude to the papal office. 'And St Peter's successor was the divinely appointed centre of unity'. This is the position which, with some qualification, was accepted by ARCIC. When Newman was studying the Donatist controversy in the early Church one phrase from St Augustine kept ringing in his ears: 'Securus iudicat orbis terrarum.' The whole world dwells secure when Rome has pronounced. It made Newman believe that Catholic truth was to be discovered not solely by appeal to the ancient and undivided Church but by the judgement of Rome. It made him think that the Roman assessment of the Church of England would be found to be right after all. Now, however, the Anglican Church itself is feeling its way towards the idea of a 'divinely appointed centre of unity'. For the ARCIC documents envisage a Catholic and Apostolic Church uniting around the see of Rome, whose particular gift it is to provide this service for the Church as a whole. Nor can the ARCIC documents be dismissed as the expression of opinion of only one, Anglo-Catholic, school of thought within the Church of England. The commission itself was representative, including at least one Anglican Evangelical, and the documents have been formally welcomed by the first Anglican Evangelical Assembly, a new body representing all the major Evangelical bodies within the Church.

Both churches have changed; both churches are on the move. If this option had seemed remotely likely to Newman we can judge he would have remained within the Church of England, speeding up the coming together. This is not a sentimental piece of wishful thinking. The fact is that Newman hated what he called private judgement, individual initiative apart from the Church as a whole. In 1841 he wrote to a Roman Catholic friend:

> What one's duty would be under other circumstances, what our duty ten or twenty years ago, I cannot say; but I do think that there is less of private judgement in going with one's Church, than in leaving it. I can earnestly desire a union between my Church and yours. I cannot listen to the thought of your being joined by individuals among us.[2]

Because of the Oxford Movement, because of Newman himself, what he desired so much, 'a union between my Church and yours', is nearer than it was. Because of what the Oxford Movement helped to recover for Anglicanism, a sense of the Church as a body under divine authority, it is appropriate to work for a union of the churches rather than thinking in terms of the movements of individuals.

Notes

CHAPTER 1 Authority – a dangerous but essential idea

1 Helmut Thielicke, *Theological Ethics*, vol. II (A. and C. Black 1969).
2 J.H. Newman, *Lectures on the Prophetical Office of the Church viewed relatively to Romanism and Popular Protestantism* (London, 1837), p. 161.
3 Ibid., p. 164.
4 L. Wittgenstein, *On Certainty* (Blackwell, 1969), sections 115, and 160.
5 *Believing in the Church* (SPCK, 1981), p. 2.
6 D.H. Lawrence, *The Rainbow* (Heinemann Phoenix edition, 1957), p. 282.
7 *The Church and the Bomb: Nuclear Weapons and Christian Conscience* (Hodder and Stoughton, 1981), p. 139.

CHAPTER 2 What is revealed

1 Philip Toynbee, *Part of a Journey* (Collins, 1982).
2 I have tried to say something about why there should be a special revelation of God in Christ, in addition to a general revelation of God in and through all things, in *Being a Christian* (Mowbray, 1981).
3 J.H. Newman, *An Essay on the Development of Christian Doctrine* (Penguin, 1974), p. 100.

CHAPTER 3 The authority of the Bible

1 'Attending to Scripture', in *Believing in the Church* (SPCK, 1981), p. 44.
2 See John Coulson, *Religion and Imagination* (Clarendon Press, 1981).

3 'Gospel Truth', in *Ways of Reading the Bible*, ed. Michael Wadsworth (The Harvester Press, 1981), p. 41.
4 In *Believing in the Church*, p. 190.
5 A review in *The Sunday Times* of *The Great Code: the Bible and Literature*, by Northrop Frye, 1982.
6 *Ways of Reading the Bible*, p. 47.
7 Karl Barth, *Evangelical Theology* (Weidenfeld and Nicholson, London, 1963), p. 160.
8 E.M. Carr, *What is History?* (Penguin, 1981), p. 30.
9 J.I. Packer, *Freedom, Authority and Scripture* (IVP, 1982), p. 57.
10 W.J. Abraham, *The Divine Inspiration of Holy Scripture* (OUP, 1981), p. 1.
11 Ibid., p. 64.
12 T.G.A. Baker, *What is the New Testament?* (SCM, 1969), p. 112.
13 John Knox, *The Early Church and the Coming Great Church* (1957), p. 49.
14 Evelyn Waugh, *Helena* (Penguin, 1978), p. 145.

CHAPTER 4 The authority of conscience

1 J.H. Newman, *Difficulties of Anglicans*, vol. 2. Letter to the Duke of Norfolk, section 5.
2 Ibid. Newman's view of conscience is not entirely clear. See D. Nicholls, 'Gladstone, Newman and Pluralism', in *Newman and Gladstone*, ed. J. Bastable, (Veritas, 1978), p. 33. On the one hand conscience must always be followed. On the other hand a Catholic has a clear duty to obey the teaching of the Church. On any specific issue which duty is paramount?

CHAPTER 5 The authority of tradition

1 J.H. Newman, *Lectures on the Prophetical Office of the Church viewed relatively to Romanism and Popular Protestantism*, p. 168.
2 Ibid., p. 170.
3 Owen Chadwick, *The Mind of the Oxford Movement* (A. and C. Black, 1963), p. 38.
4 Ibid., p. 39.
5 *Selected Prose of T.S. Eliot*, ed. Frank Kermode (Faber and Faber, 1975), p. 38.
6 A.M. Allchin, *The Dynamic of Tradition* (DLT, 1981), p. 28.

7 *The Mind of the Oxford Movement*, p. 41.
8 W. Palmer, *Treatise on the Church*, quoted in *The Mind of the Oxford Movement*, p. 131.
9 ARCIC, A I, 18.
10 Christopher Butler, *The Theology of Vatican 2* (DLT, 1967), p. 43.
11 Keble, *Nine Sermons Preached before the University of Oxford*, quoted in *The Mind of the Oxford Movement*, p. 130.
12 *The Theology of Vatican 2*, pp. 44–5.
13 *Lectures on the Prophetical Office*, p. 62.
14 Ibid., pp. 264–7.
15 William Palmer, *Treatise on the Church*, quoted in *The Mind of the Oxford Movement*, p. 133.

CHAPTER 6 Infallibility and the mind of the faithful

1 *Lectures on the Prophetical Office*, p. 225.
2 Ibid., p. 232.
3 Ibid., p. 249.
4 Ibid., p. 252.
5 J.H. Newman, *An Essay on the Development of Christian Doctrine* (Penguin, 1974), p. 100.
6 Ibid., p. 142.
7 *The Documents of Vatican 2*, ed. Walter M. Abott (Chapman, 1966), II, 8. p. 116.
8 Christopher Butler, *The Theology of Vatican 2* (DLT, 1967), p. 40.
9 ARCIC, A II, 32, n. 7.
10 H. Kung, *Infallible?* (Fount, 1977), p. 142.
11 Geoffrey Wainwright, *Doxology, A Systematic Theology* (Epworth, 1980), p. 438.
12 *The Documents of Vatican 2*, p. 29.
13 *The Theology of Vatican 2*, p. 25.
14 Quoted in *Infallible?* p. 150.
15 Timothy Ware, *The Orthodox Church* (Penguin, 1963), p. 255.
16 Ibid.
17 ARCIC, A II, 23.
18 ARCIC, A II, 25.
19 *The Times*, 28 May 1982.
20 The reference is to ARCIC, A II, 29.
21 *The Documents of Vatican 2*, II, 10, p. 117.

CHAPTER 7 Indefectibility and infallibility

1 H. Kung, *Infallible?* (Fount, 1977), p. 153.
2 See W. Pannenberg, *Jesus God and Man* (SCM, 1968), pp. 183–7. To say that Christian doctrines are doxological does not mean that they have no objective reference or that they function simply as expressions of emotion and to arouse similar emotions in others. They assert what is claimed to be the case; but the reality to which they refer is not an object of knowledge to be manipulated. This reality, God, can only be properly known as an object of praise.
3 Hilary of Poitiers, *De Trinitate*, 11, 2.
4 'On the Concept of Infallibility in Catholic Theology', *Theological Investigations*, vol. 4 (DLT, 1976), p. 66.
5 Rodney Needham, *Belief, Language and Experience* (Blackwell, 1972), pp. 24, 65.
6 In his essay 'On the Concept of Infallibility in Catholic Theology'.
7 Austin Farrer, 'Infallibility and Historical Revelation', in *Interpretation and Belief* SPCK, (1976), pp. 162, 164.

CHAPTER 8 The Anglican heritage

1 'ARCIC and the Papacy', in MC, the journal of the Modern Churchman's Union, New Series, vol. xxv, No. 1.
2 'The Authority of the First Four General Councils in the Anglican Communion', *Anglican Theological Review*, April 1962.
3 Dean Church, *Occasional Papers*, vol. III, p. 393.
4 Christopher Butler, *The Theology of Vatican 2* (DLT, 1967), p. 106.

POSTSCRIPT: Newman, Rome and the task today

1 Meriol Trevor, *Newman's Journey* (Fount, 1977), p. 112.
2 Newman, *Apologia Pro Vita Sua* (Fontana, 1959), p. 239.

Index